Extraordinary Date Night Ideas

52 Budget-Friendly Activities to Strengthen and Recharge Your Relationship, Rekindle Intimacy, and Build Trust

Monica Bacchus

© **Copyright 2022 by Monica Bacchus- All rights reserved.**

The content contained within this book may not be reproduced, duplicated or transmitted without direct written permission from the author or the publisher.

Under no circumstances will any blame or legal responsibility be held against the publisher, or author, for any damages, reparation, or monetary loss due to the information contained within this book, either directly or indirectly.

Legal Notice:

This book is copyright protected. It is only for personal use. You cannot amend, distribute, sell, use, quote, or paraphrase any part, or the content within this book, without the consent of the author or publisher.

Disclaimer Notice:

Please note that the information contained within this document is for educational and entertainment purposes only. All effort has been executed to present accurate, up-to-date, reliable, complete information. No warranties of any kind are declared or implied. Readers acknowledge that the author is not engaged in the rendering of legal, financial, medical, or professional advice. The content within this book has been derived from various sources. Please consult a licensed professional before attempting any techniques outlined in this book.

By reading this document, the reader agrees that under no circumstances is the author responsible for any losses, direct or indirect, that are incurred as a result of the use of the information contained within this document, including, but not limited to, errors, omissions, or inaccuracies.

CONTENTS

Introduction   7

Part I
LOVE CONQUERS ALL

1. CONSIDER YOURSELF LUCKY   15
   You and Your Partner   18
   The Power of Love   23
   Story: The Healing Power of Love   25
   Moving on...   26

2. NEVER SAY NO TO A DATE   27
   Reasons to Work on Your Relationship   30
   Why Couples Need to Go on Dates   32
   Preparation   34
   Moving on...   35

Part II
THE DATE ACTIVITIES

3. THE CREATIVE ACTIVITIES   39
   Date Number 1: Creative Cooking   40
   Date Number 2: Weird Painting   42
   Date Number 3: Dance Moves   44
   Date Number 4: Sitcom Date   48
   Date Number 5: Bartending Date   49
   Date Number 6: ABC Date   51
   Date Number 7: Menu Creation   52
   Date Number 8: Imaginary Wedding   54
   Date Number 9: Memory Lane   55
   Date Number 10: Secret Code   56
   Moving on...   58

4. **THE ADVENTUROUS ACTIVITIES** — 59
   Date Number 11: Random Cards — 61
   Date Number 12: Choose A Destination — 62
   Date Number 13: Virtual Concert — 63
   Date Number 14: Partner's Choice — 64
   Date Number 15: Wild Cards — 64
   Date Number 16: Cyber Date — 67
   Date Number 17: Park Date — 71
   Date Number 18: Scavenger Hunt — 72
   Date Number 19: Plant Together — 73
   Date Number 20: The Long Walk — 75
   Moving on... — 77

5. **THE PERSONAL ACTIVITIES** — 79
   Date Number 21: Alternative Ending — 80
   Date Number 22: Popcorn and Romance — 81
   Date Number 23: Lovely Adjectives — 82
   Date Number 24: Happy Medium — 84
   Date Number 25: A New Life — 85
   Date Number 26: Imagine That — 86
   Date Number 27: The Love Story — 88
   Date Number 28: Quiet Date — 90
   Date Number 29: Bucket List — 91
   Date Number 30: The Spa Date — 93
   Date Number 31: Dream Board — 95
   Moving on... — 97

6. **THE PLAYFUL ACTIVITIES** — 99
   Date Number 32: Mystery Taste-Testing — 100
   Date Number 33: Total Stranger — 101
   Date Number 34: Game Night — 103
   Date Number 35: State the States — 106
   Date Number 36: The Book Date — 107
   Date Number 37: Fantasy Game — 109
   Date Number 38: Silent Movie Date — 110
   Date Number 39: Puzzle Date — 111
   Date Number 40: New Hobby Together — 113

Date Number 41: Match Game	115
Date Number 42: New Address	116
Date Number 43: Bedroom Picnic	118
Moving on...	120
7. THE CRAZY ACTIVITIES	121
Date Number 44: The $10 Date	123
Date Number 45: Conjoined Baker	124
Date Number 46: Dancing Challenge	126
Date Number 47: Show and Tell	127
Date Number 48: Guess What	128
Date Number 49: Difficult Date	130
Date Number 50: Candid Camera	133
Date Number 51: Crazy Fun	135
Date Number 52: The Boxes	136
Moving on...	138

Part III
LOVE RUNS THROUGH THE
STOMACH

8. THE DATE NIGHT MEALS	141
One Dish Roast Pork	143
Shrimp Risotto	147
Chicken Parmesan	150
Slow Cooked Beef Stew	151
Rainbow Vegetable Curry	153
Salmon en Papillote	155
Creamy Baked Macaroni and Cheese	157
Mushroom Stroganoff	159
Beef Ragu	160
Turkey Burgers	162
Moving On...	163
9. THE DATE NIGHT DESSERTS AND DRINKS	165
Cheesecake for Two	166
Individual Strawberry Trifles	168

Chocolate Mousse	170
Red Velvet Mug Cake	172
Molten Chocolate Cake for Two	174
The Magic of Cocktails	176
Moving on…	183
Conclusion	185
Supporting Information Lists	189
Bibliography	193

INTRODUCTION

Being deeply loved by someone gives you strength while loving someone deeply gives you courage.
–Lao Tzu

Dating, though daunting, is rewarding and fun. We dress up, dab on some of our best fragrances, and enjoy good food, drinks, and company. It sounds simple enough. It is… until you are married, have a couple of children, a demanding schedule, and countless responsibilities. In the past, for our parents and grandparents, the challenges in dating were different. There were fewer options, so dinner and a movie, a visit to a drive-in, a milkshake cafe, or a fun fair were obvious go-to options. But today, we are bombarded with information on the internet, and social media is constantly upping the stakes in what is considered a pleasing date. We want more for ourselves and our partners, pushing to create better experiences.

Some people would tell you that *The Notebook* is the most remarkable love story. Still, its protagonists—Noah and Allie—did not have an easy go of things together during their relationship. The movie teaches us that as long as we are committed to doing whatever it takes for each other, we can build something powerful and beautiful together. It is usual for couples to experience challenges or setbacks, but how the two of you choose to deal with those experiences will make you stronger.

So it's not gonna be easy. It's going to be really hard; we're gonna have to work at this every day, but I want to do that because I want you. I want all of you, forever, every day. You and me... every day. –Noah, Nicholas Sparks, *The Notebook*

Despite the odds of finding love, you have done it—you found that one person you love more than anyone else in the world. Love has incredible power to improve your lives, both emotionally and physically. Documented benefits of experiencing a loving relationship include:

- improving your broader social skills
- becoming a happier person
- becoming a more patient person
- increasing confidence and feeling of security
- improving your immune system
- improving heart health and blood pressure
- living longer

You remember the butterflies you felt when you first met and the passion for each other at the start, and now you wish you could keep that feeling forever. It is usual for the novelty of a new relationship to eventually wear off and leave us feeling like everything has become predictable. You slip easily into autopilot in your relationships because it helps you navigate the things around you and your daily responsibilities more efficiently. You get into routines, like brushing your teeth the same way every morning or eating the same things because it is simple and quick; you even claim the same side of the bed every night. For any relationship to remain healthy and vibrant, it takes work from both parties involved; breaking your mundane routines will help you appreciate each other. As long as you still want your partner, there is hope that you can rekindle your early spark.

Similarly, you have adapted to your partner's expectations and daily habits. They switch into autopilot too, and it becomes easy to take their contributions for granted. Suppose you listen to your partner carefully and refresh your understanding of whom you share your life with. In that case, you will see a dramatic positive shift in your relationship.

The idea of extra effort can seem stressful, especially if you and your partner both have busy schedules and younger children that need looking after. However, once you take the first step and block out some time together to work out a plan of action, the rest will flow more smoothly. The payoff is also worth far more than the initial investment of time. The benefits of treating each other to regular date nights include:

- helping to maintain a healthy relationship
- keeping your spark alive or rekindling it together
- creating a time when the two of you can be together without distractions
- improving your understanding of one another
- reducing stress for both of you
- strengthens your bond

It is best to act before a relationship is on the rocks before acting to save it. Prevention will always have a better outcome than a cure; it is much easier. If you feel things have been slowing down lately, take steps to recharge yourselves and nurture even more intimacy.

It is easy to feel stuck if you are concerned that your date nights together are not what they used to be. Perhaps the activities do not feel as exciting as they once were. You may want to know how to change it, especially if neither of you is trying to keep your date nights like you used to.

Taking the initiative to dedicate your time and attention to your partner again will make them feel valued, like they are your top priority, and remember why they love you too. Instead of feeling daunted about addressing problems, create anticipation and get excited about spending quality time together away from any stressors you both have. Couples that invest their time in each other's happiness are less likely to experience breakups—they can even live longer.

There is one significant factor: Love is the catalyst that brought the two of you together, and fostering that love can re-invigorate your date nights.

So what is the key to unlocking the benefits of spending this time together? Regular date nights!

There are 52 inspiring ideas for date nights in this book. There are 20 recipe ideas for main courses, desserts, and drinks you can make together. By pairing these ideas and choosing a new activity to try each week, you can reap the benefits, rekindle your love for each other, and grow the magic of your shared connection.

So do not delay. Take a leaf from Noah's romantic ideas in *The Notebook*, and commit to going the extra mile for one another today. Read on to get inspiration and instructions for many date nights.

But despite their differences, they had one important thing in common... They were crazy about each other.
–Duke, Nicholas Sparks, *The Notebook*

PART I

LOVE CONQUERS ALL

1

CONSIDER YOURSELF LUCKY

So, I love you because the entire universe conspired to help me find you. –Paulo Coelho, *The Alchemist*

When life is hectic and demanding, it is hard to feel enthusiastic about love life. However, according to psychology, you and your partner are some of the lucky ones. The chances of meeting any one person are meager. In 2020 the world population was 7.7 billion; even if you think on a smaller scale about your likelihood of meeting your partner, the population of the United States of America in the same year was 331 million (Worldometers.info, 2022). Despite billions of people, you found your way to each other and fell in love. You beat the odds.

That love you feel for each other is more than just a warm fuzzy feeling in your heart in the early days of your relationship. There are emotional and physical benefits to being in love in the longer term. Did you know that these benefits can even go as far as helping you live longer? Studies have found that married people live longer than singles (Tanzi, 2019).

Some other widely accepted benefits of finding a loving relationship include:

- Love decreases physical pain.
- Love makes you a better person.
- Marriage is beneficial to your health.
- Love alters your sense of taste.
- Being in love affects your ability to focus.

It is worth occasionally reminding yourself why you are lucky to have what you have in your relationship and why it is worth holding onto it with everything you can give. Even if you put aside its psychological and physical benefits, the two of you are still some of the fortunate few.

Some say you view the world through rose-colored glasses when you are in love, and the world tastes sweeter. It is an old wives' tale, but those ancient soothsayers may have been onto something. Being in love can alter both your ability to focus and the way you taste things. Food is perceived as sweeter when you feel or think about love, and the teasing you may get from your friends and family about being distracted reflects a tendency for those in love to spend time thinking about their partners when they are apart.

You do not necessarily need to have your partner at your side 24/7 to experience the benefits of being in love. Looking at photographs of loved ones or holding their hands can reduce the experience of physical pain, suggesting that the mere knowledge of having social support from your partner is enough to positively impact your experience during traumatic events (Wilbert & Chang, 2009).

Perhaps, you have heard People describe their partners as their "better half," but there is more truth to this expression than a simple joke when meeting new people. Though, it is less about your partner being better than you and more a case of you making each other better people. One study of 245 young couples found that being in a relationship can speed up natural personality development and reduce neuroticism as the individuals showed less tendency to view ambiguous situations negatively (Finn et al., 2015).

YOU AND YOUR PARTNER

Your partner is with you because they love you just as deeply as you love them. The pride and awe you feel for them reflect how they see you. Remember that your partner is proud of you and genuinely wants to spend time with you. They enjoy being in your company, and you deserve to receive their affection as much as you want to lavish them with yours. To keep that spark glowing requires you to work at it, but no one says you cannot have fun while you continue developing your relationship.

Having a partner in your life—someone to share in your shenanigans and be there to support your daily grind—has its merits, even if you are not married.

Benefit One: Having Someone by Your Side Makes You a Happier Person

The body produces many hormones for countless reasons, but a few regulate your mood and create feelings of happiness. Oxytocin is commonly referred to as the "love hormone" because it is responsible for feeling connected to other people. You generate this hormone when you make physical contact with your partner, and you can up its levels by holding hands, hugging, kissing, and having sex. This hormone also promotes empathy and can help you build trust in relationships. Theoretically, we could embrace our way to more secure bonds with our partners and feel happier.

Benefit Two: Having a Partner Makes You More Confident and Secure

The Dreamworks animated movie *Shrek* is an unconventional love story. Still, it is more relatable than most because the characters display acts of bravery that they would never have considered had they not met one another. Spoiler alert if you have not seen it yet: Shrek wants to impress Princess Fiona and ultimately gets outside his comfort zone to rescue her, whereas the princess learns to be confident in her appearance and be true to herself. The movie is an excellent portrayal of how the support and affection of a loving partner can give you the bravery to live confidently.

Benefit Three: Stress Is Less When You Have a Partner

When you are in a healthy partnership, you support each other, including being a sounding board after a tough work day or helping cheer each other up when you are down. Remember that select group of mood-regulating hormones? They play a part here too. Endorphins are a group of hormones that relieve stress and are commonly known as the "feel-good" hormones. Dopamine is a hormone responsible for making you feel pleasure; it also helps increase your motivation and memory. The saying that "laughter is the best medicine" certainly applies to these hormones, as both are released when you laugh—so spending an enjoyable time with your partner will reduce stress's effects.

Benefit Four: You Have Someone Who Can Help You Learn Right From Wrong

Sometimes the people around you may avoid the subjects they think are sensitive. Perhaps they are too frightened to tell you when they feel you are wrong. An honest partner, though, will let you know when they think you are not behaving in the best way. Your partner wants you to succeed and will not stop letting you know when they feel you have done something wrong. After all, if you are never made aware of your mistakes, how would you learn from them and grow. Their input helps you understand when you may have crossed a line or how to do better next time.

Benefit Five: With a Partner, You Can Discover More About Yourself

Spending time together at the beginning of a relationship can help you figure out whether this person is the one you want to stay with indefinitely. When you spend time with your partner, you develop a sense of what you want from your partner and how you want to give and receive love. It helps you uncover attitudes or personality traits that you would not have had the opportunity to cultivate alone.

Benefit Six: It Helps You Become a Patient Person

All relationships come with their fair share of obstacles you must learn to navigate to flourish together. It could be that your relationship is long distance, your work schedules conflict, or your backgrounds are so different that you often misunderstand each other's viewpoints. Working through these things can take work, compromise, and a willingness to wait for the efforts to pay off. You will learn to be patient with yourself, your shared goals, and your partner as you work through each obstacle together.

Benefit Seven: You Have Someone to Take Care of You and Check on You

When you are sick or feeling down, it is natural to hope that a loved one can provide support. When you are in a relationship, your partner will often perform seemingly small acts that speak volumes about how much they care for you. Have you ever had them remind you to take a precautionary raincoat, stay hydrated, take your medication on time, or even bring the medication directly to you when you are under the weather? Your partner becomes a barometer for your well-being, reminding you to get the daily essentials done and checking in on you when you forget to prioritize yourselves.

Benefit Eight: You Have More Encouragement and a Cheerleader

When you are in a healthy relationship, you are more successful. A loving partner will be more than willing to take a back seat to your dreams and goals during crunch time. They allow you the space to focus on your dreams. They will actively champion your efforts at self-improvement, like your own personal cheerleader. They are proud of your accomplishments and the work you put in to get there. They shout the loudest when it is time to celebrate your success, but they are also there when things do not go to plan, encouraging you to keep trying and boosting your motivation.

Benefit Nine: You Have a Team to Plan for the Future

Your partner does not just champion you in parts of your life where your goals overlap with how you live together; they become teammates in planning for a brighter future. Shared goal-building with your partner is very rewarding and gives you an ally in your efforts to get what you want out of life. With you and your partner working toward the same goals, you can achieve them twice as quickly and enjoy the benefits together. Whether you dream of buying a house or organizing a year of traveling the world you have always wanted, having a teammate in saving, organizing, and ultimately achieving it makes the rewards double the fun.

THE POWER OF LOVE

Young or new couples are not the only ones to experience the benefits of a partnership—a healthy long-term marriage also benefits your physical health. Married people have improved heart health and a boosted immune system and are more likely to book and keep medical appointments due to the extra support from their partner. The experience of being in love is compelling; with all those hormones zipping about and the increased likelihood that you will look after each other and yourselves, it becomes easier to understand how these facts can be true. Here are some of the wonders that love can create in your body.

You Can Live Longer

Living longer is particularly relevant for you if you are a man. Some studies suggest that married men have better recovery rates from illnesses or surgical treatments than unmarried men and live ten years longer on average (Naik, 2011). A reduction in stress and a motivation to keep yourself healthy to continue impressing your partner may be why you develop more good habits.

Your Body Can Heal at a Faster Rate

People with a solid social support system show lower levels of the stress hormone cortisol than those who do not have access to such support. Doctors suggest this can contribute to the increased recovery rate of people who have active help from their friends and family. Having your partner there to support you emotionally and physically during a time of ill health will reduce the time it takes you to get back on your feet.

Love Can Lower Your Blood Pressure

Have you heard of broken heart syndrome? It is a condition where people experience physical pain at the loss of a loved one; debatably, it is also attributed as one of the possible causes of a heart attack. The opposite effect can be true when you have a presence of love and a partner with whom you are highly connected. When coupled with reducing stress for people in love, it is easy to understand why your blood pressure will decrease if you feel loved.

Love Can Improve Your Immune System

Speaking of stress, doctors have linked ongoing stress to declining health and a lowered immune system. If love can reduce stress levels, it can also improve your immune function.

Love Can Help Make Your Heart Healthier

Love gives your heart plenty of exercises. The fluttering you feel when your loved one is near is not a solely emotional response—it is physical too. When you feel love, your brain releases dopamine, adrenaline, and norepinephrine; these hormones speed up your heart rate and strengthen your heart.

STORY: THE HEALING POWER OF LOVE

We often witness the incredible healing power of love in our lives. Plenty of medical staff have stories of everyday miracles enacted through love. The following story is just one example; it is the experience of Christopher D. Connors and was first published on the website "P.S. I Love You" in 2019.

In his article, Christopher recalls how he was heartbroken to receive the news that a close friend's son had been diagnosed with cancer. At the time, his friend had asked for prayers, love, and unity in requesting healing for their three-year-old son.

The following two years after the diagnosis, Christopher witnessed his friends and their families displaying incredible hope, faith, positivity, and determination while helping their toddler battle for his life. Now, the child is officially cancer-free.

The love witnessed by all who surrounded the family also had a ripple effect; it inspired those in proximity to looking at what matters to them in their own lives. It prompted Christopher to reflect on how beautiful it is to be charitable and compassionate to others and the tremendous healing power of love.

MOVING ON...

In this chapter, we looked at how experiencing love can benefit you, how having a partner contributes to making you a better person, and how love has the innate power to physically and emotionally strengthen you.

Chapter two adds to this to discuss why dates or the act of going on dates—with your partner in particular—can help you build on that power to strengthen and heal. The next chapter will discuss how you can pull all of these benefits to the forefront and bring that power to life, using regular date night activities with your partner as a conduit to strengthen and recharge your relationship.

2

NEVER SAY NO TO A DATE

Some think dating is just a way to woo a potential new partner, but the real reason we do it is to get to know one another. The purest intimacy is often had when you open yourself up, enjoy each other's company, and be present in the moment. It is just as meaningful for long-term healthy relationships as it is when we start a new one. A well-planned date can be just as exciting as indulging in spontaneity together—and honestly, who does not like to feel that they are the most significant thing in their partner's world?

In 2018, Buzzfeed collected the experiences of its community users, and ten of the shared sweetest stories made it into an article by Ali Velez. Three of those stories contained something personal to each couple. They show how the level of effort, from meticulous planning to a spur-of-the-moment decision, can be just as incredible. The stories are also great examples of the power of spending that time together and bonding.

One user recounted when a date she went on turned into a sunset flight across her hometown. She may not have known this was going to take place, but her date for the evening had undoubtedly put some extra thought into the date. It probably seems a little cheesy that their date was aeronautically themed when he is a pilot by profession, but he was laying the foundation for the night's culmination. They spent the evening dining at a restaurant near the runways to watch planes take off and land. The user was surprised when the date escorted her for a personal flying lesson after dinner. She remembers the experience of getting to see the sunset from that plane as "the best first date I'd ever been on!" (Velez, 2018)

What made this particular date stand out is the man's effort to share a part of himself with his date. You can see from the story that the love of planes and being a pilot must be significant to him, and he lets his new date in on that part of his life beautifully and romanticly.

The second story is a far less organized experience, but it still showed a level of effort on the part of the woman sharing it that revealed to her date just how thoughtful and caring she is. The storyteller met a man through some mutual friends and had heard that it was his birthday. She called him on the day and sang the Happy Birthday song across the line. The birthday wishes shocked him but also made him very happy, especially since he shared that she had been the first person to share the celebration with him that day. As the conversation continued, she discovered that he would be alone for the day, so she invited him to dinner that evening. She had no time to prepare a gift, so instead, she got a cupcake for their dessert, put a candle in it, and sang to him again. It may have been their first evening together, but the thoughtfulness she displayed that night went a long way, as the couple is now married.

The last one is a movie romance dialed up to 100 and brought to life. This user recalls a date when she had a wonderful dinner, during which she and her date had zoned entirely out everyone else in the restaurant while they talked for hours. After dinner, they returned to his home, where he made her a hot toddy and continued talking. Eventually, they shared a sweet kiss. You might think their date could not have gone any smoother, but the man in this story has more to offer. He asks his date if she would like to dance with him, and she recalls the feeling that she had been "plopped into a Nicholas Sparks movie" (Velez, 2018). They danced among fairy lights in his bedroom while music softly played and shared another good night kiss on her front porch after he drove her home. When the user shared this story, they had recently celebrated their fifth anniversary.

REASONS TO WORK ON YOUR RELATIONSHIP

It is easy sometimes to feel a little uninspired when things go smoothly. Maintaining a healthy relationship can be a challenging act of balance and compromise. Remember that disagreements happen, and you can always work on your partnership to make it stronger and more exciting. Below is a list of why working things out or making your bond tighter is worth the extra effort. Furthermore, as you saw on romantic dates, that effort can sometimes be as little as a phone call on a particular day. The idea is to ensure that whatever you do builds something great between you and makes your partner feel valued.

- Reason one: You love each other. When two people are not suitable for each other, there is a multitude of signs that you cannot ignore. However, if you still feel like your world would not be complete without your partner, you are

most likely still in love. Finding such a special connection with someone is hard, and it is worth trying to rekindle the passion from your early days together.
- Reason two: You have invested time together. The two of you have already done the groundwork, got to know each other, built a life together, and may even have shared investments, pets, or children. It is important to remember why you love each other in the first place.
- Reason three: You both want to rekindle the magic. It takes two to tango, as the adage says. So if your partner has indicated that they want to work with you to make things better again, you will have greater chances of pulling it off together.
- Reason four: You will both do whatever it takes. Once you have decided to work on recharging your relationship batteries, you will need to recognize that the process might include some uncomfortable conversations. You may have bad habits that your partner feels are harming you or both of you. In these cases, you may be willing to lose that habit as a part of your life to replace it with a much healthier relationship.

- Reason five: You are a team and okay with being vulnerable with each other. When you and your partner commit to rediscovering your magic, addressing any of your concerns will be much more palatable. It can be painful to talk through problems, but if you are willing to open yourself up and be vulnerable, you can support each other and feel great hope. You have worked through things in the past and can do it again.
- Reason six: You still have fun together and want to improve the relationship for the future. Life always comes with challenges and can throw plenty of stress your way. You and your partner can quickly work through these things together and have fun to stave off the pressure of everyday life. That fun is an excellent foundation for continuing to improve your relationship.

WHY COUPLES NEED TO GO ON DATES

Spending time together helps maintain your relationship. Do not leave it until there is a decline; maintenance is just as essential to keep the joy of your relationship before it ebbs away. Dedicating some time with no outside distractions can lead to in-depth conversations and continuing to learn new things about each other, even if you have been together for a long time. Having fun together and actively putting effort into genuinely being present for your partner can rekindle your spark.

When both partners are willing to go the extra mile to make a success of a shared activity on a date, it increases the level of fondness that you have for one another and helps you understand how to be more attentive in everyday life outside of your dates. When your schedules are busy, it can feel like a mammoth task to find the time when both of you are free, but you will be surprised how many small portions of time there are in your week that you can take advantage of once you start to look for it. Having dedicated time helps to encourage you both to make the most of the experience. Even if you are not feeling stuck or concerned about your relationship, spending quality time together can still improve the quality of your relationship by strengthening your connection.

Married couples who regularly go on date nights stay together longer than those who do not and experience greater levels of intimacy with each other. Date nights can improve communication with your partner, especially if you both choose to make your date a tech-free zone. The novelty of stepping outside the ordinary can encourage you to enjoy the fun of the experience, especially if you have been bored or feel your relationship is predictable.

Putting each other first will help you recapture the magic of your love for one another. It can strengthen your commitment to one another as you get into the habit of spending time with each other on dates. The reduction in stress that comes with regular date nights can make you feel happier, and this happiness is often associated with time spent with one another.

PREPARATION

There is an old saying, "if you fail to prepare, then you are preparing to fail." Although there is value in impromptu dates, planning is essential, especially when you are just starting your dating journey together. Here are some tips for making the most of an excellent preparation strategy:

- Schedule at least 30 minutes together so you can plan your date without interruptions.
- Bring your calendars! It does not matter if it is digital or on paper, but you will need them to help you decide which dates and times every week suit you both.

- Commit to scheduling date nights for at least 20 weeks.
- Make the dates your priority. Once you have planned your schedule, if either of you has an event or meeting that you have to attend, decline based on the fact that you already have an appointment on that day that you cannot change: your date.
- You can pick out the activities you want to try together each week in advance or choose one from the list on the day of each date, but keep trying new things.
- Refer to the suggested items on the dates listed in upcoming chapters to be sure you have everything you need ahead of time.
- The list of suggested recipes is a great starting point, but you should also try to use your imagination for more recipes or adjust them to suit your tastes.
- Set conversation rules before you start. Consider banning discussions about work, politics, the kids, or finances unless it is part of the date activity. Remind each other about your upcoming date regularly; create a sense of anticipation and excitement for your time together.

MOVING ON...

Now that you understand the importance of keeping up a date night schedule and its power to help you both take your relationship to new heights, you are ready to move on to the next stage: the date night ideas!

Part two of this book will present ideas for your date night activities, suggested items, and optional extras.

PART II

THE DATE ACTIVITIES

3

THE CREATIVE ACTIVITIES

Love can make you more creative; a study in the Netherlands suggests that feelings of love can stimulate global processing in the brain, which aligns with the brain activation caused by the presence of dopamine (Förster et al., 2018, p.1479-91). There is a thought that the dopamine released when you experience a romantic connection stimulates long-term thinking and increased creativity. The study tested this by assessing participants' creativity and analytical ability. They had to imagine walking with a loved one—or their ideal partner if they were single. Following the imagined walk, they retook the test. The results concluded that thinking of a romantic partner could increase your creativity.

This chapter gives you ten date night ideas to practice your creativity together and activate that long-term focus in your brains while still having fun.

DATE NUMBER 1: CREATIVE COOKING

Get ready to turn an ordinary evening of cooking dinner into a memorable experience. Challenge each other and practice creativity, communication, and patience. The experience is more fun if you have different food tastes and one of you is not a better cook.

Suggested Equipment

- herbs, spices, and salt
- cooking oil of your choice
- at least ten ingredients from your fridge or pantry
- appropriate pots, pans

Date Instructions

1. Each person should select five ingredients from the fridge or the pantry. You will want to choose at least one protein and some vegetables. Your protein does not have to be meat, so feel free to adapt the challenge to suit any diet.

2. Once you have ten ingredients, you must restrict yourselves from adding more besides seasonings.

3. Set the scene by playing upbeat music you enjoy while cooking.

4. Work together to create a meal using your selected ingredients. Be creative and avoid falling back on simple meat and vegetable dish. To be successful at the challenge, you must use all ten ingredients; though you can't pick extra ingredients, you can go wild with herbs and seasoning instead.

5. Take time to set the table for two. It is a date! Choose a nice table center, bring out your best china or use paper plates. Consider adding some candles; if you are a fan of scented candles, choose a soft, romantic scent like rose or jasmine. You want to avoid selecting scents that will overwhelm the aroma of your cooking.

6. Change your music before you settle down together to eat; opt for something more subdued and play it at a low volume so you can engage in conversation over dinner.

7. Consider implementing some rules to keep your attention on your date. Don't be tempted to turn on the TV—even if it is only for background noise—and leave your phones in another room if possible.

8. Cleaning up is just as important, so don't leave it all to your partner alone or do everything yourself. Cleaning as you go is a good idea, but consider how fast you can get through it after dinner if you both work together. Sharing this chore might seem tedious, but it will make you feel more supported, especially if one of you usually does a larger share of the housework.

DATE NUMBER 2: WEIRD PAINTING

This date aims to create maximum space for you and your partner to relax in each other's company. It's about getting as creative as possible together and breaking any preconceived rules you may have about making artwork. It will require a small amount of preparation beforehand, but that is all the better for building excitement for your date while you gather your resources for the night.

Suggested Equipment

- decorators, dust sheets, or old bedsheets that you no longer use
- a canvas or another large surface for painting
- a variety of colorful paints
- paint brushes and sponges
- any items that make interesting shapes or patterns when used as a stamp

- other pattern-making tools, such as pouring pots, stencils, or scrapers
- a jar of water to wash your brushes
- some old clothing that you wouldn't mind getting ruined by paint

Date Instructions

1. If you don't already have paint supplies, take a shopping trip together to choose some and remind each other during the journey about how exciting it is to plan something creative. Be sure to select acrylic or other water-based paints.

2. Work with your partner to think up some items you don't mind getting covered in paint to use as exciting stamps. Alternatively, challenge each other to find two to five items each and bring them along on the night.

3. Choose an appropriate room to paint in; ideally, you want an empty indoor space, but if the weather permits, consider being outdoors, too.

4. Lay down your protective sheets, set up your canvas, and gather all your painting supplies into your workspace.

5. Work together to create one painting. It doesn't have to be highly planned or intricately detailed if you don't want it to be, but you should allow the process to

encourage you to play around with your materials. Try using your non-dominant hand whenever possible so that the two of you can create something fun while acknowledging your weaknesses.

6. Experiment with the colors and tools the two of you have gathered. Focus on enjoying yourselves and make use of your hands and sponges too. Don't be frightened of getting each other dirty. Water-based paints will easily wash off the skin with warm water, soap, or a facial cleanser.

7. Once you have completed your painting, allow some time to dry before you move it.

8. Keep your painting somewhere where you can view it often. It doesn't need to be in a central place in your living room if your creation together doesn't fit the style of your decor, but still choose a location where it can catch your eye while you go about your daily business.

9. Use the painting as a talking point often in the future.

DATE NUMBER 3: DANCE MOVES

Dancing together can improve your intimacy, but it also helps you and your partner practice your patience with each other and learn to take cues from your body language. The goal of this date is to get the two of you more in tune with one another while having fun together.

Suggested Equipment

- dance appropriate clothing—avoid tightly fitting items
- a music player of choice
- a selection of romantic or spicy music

Date Instructions

1. Choose some music that both of you will enjoy listening to; be prepared to hear a lot of it on repeat while you are practicing.

2. You and your partner should dress the part; getting ready for your date will add anticipation for the experience. Choose smart-casual dress as a minimum, as making an effort to dress nicely will build a feeling that something special is happening while you are getting ready.

3. Choose a room with plenty of space where you can both move freely without the danger of tripping over anything. If you will be staying at home for this date and have pets, it is also a good idea to shut them out of

the room you are in to prevent them from getting underfoot and potentially causing an accident.

4. Below are instructions for learning some basic dance steps; once you have mastered these, use them as a base from which you can experiment. Get creative and add your dance moves.

5. Another alternative is to find a lesson online and follow the instructions.

Dance Move Basics

As Johnny Castle puts it in *Dirty Dancing*, start with a frame:

> "This is my dance space, this is your dance space. I do not go into yours; you do not go into mine. You gotta hold the frame."

- Face towards one another.
- Keep your back straight and bend your knees slightly.
- For the leader: Bend your right arm at the elbow and place your hand under your partner's arm, resting your palm on the back of their shoulder blade. Hold your left arm to your

side and grasp your partner's right hand; keep your elbow bent, and remember that your clasped hands can be used as a pointer to guide your partner.
- For the follower: Bend your left arm at the elbow and place it along the top of your partner's arm; rest your hand on their shoulder. Bend your right hand at the elbow and clasp your partner's left hand.
- Both partners should hold their arms in a strong frame but not become so rigid that they feel tense.

The essential side step is the first thing you should learn, as it will form a base you can use for all other moves.

- The leader will move to the left and the follower to the right.
- Step one foot to your side and don't exaggerate your steps—smaller steps will help you keep up with more types of music.
- Bring your opposite foot across to meet the first one and transfer your weight onto that leg.
- Step out to the side again with your first foot.
- Follow your foot with your opposite leg. This time do not transfer your weight; instead, tap

your toes to the floor next to your first foot, lifting your heel slightly.
- Switch directions and repeat the above moves.
- The whole sequence fits into a count of eight beats.

Hopefully, this gets you started; you are on your own from here on. You choose if you want to create your next moves or if you are serious about learning a dance. Your decision will take you to a dance class or have you laughing and enjoying the night trying to make your special dance; either way, relax and have fun.

DATE NUMBER 4: SITCOM DATE

This date focuses on engaging your imagination. It encourages you both to take a fun look at your life and imagine how it might look if you were the stars of a sitcom. There isn't any equipment needed for this date night, so it's also a great one for times in the month when you may not want to spend money. However, at the back of the book, there is a list of some of America's favorite sitcoms that you can refer to for some ideas if you aren't sure where to begin.

Date Instructions

Work together to create an imaginary personal sitcom. Ask each other the following questions and discuss your answers; keep the date lighthearted and bring your sense of humor.

1. If your life became a sitcom, who would play the characters in your family? Don't forget to cast supporting characters such as neighbors and friends.

2. What would be your storyline? What are the things that it would center around, and why?

3. What would you name your sitcom?

Perhaps these questions will remind you of funny memories you share—moments in life that you think would show up in your sitcom. If the two of you are feeling extra creative, you could even consider creating a theme song for your show.

DATE NUMBER 5: BARTENDING DATE

This date aims to give you and your partner something fun to discover together. You could book a cocktail-making experience together or just as easily create your own bartending experience at home. The date instructions here explain what to do if you will be completing the date at home. Please be aware of your limits and drink responsibility if you include alcoholic ingredients.

Suggested Equipment

- a variety of ingredients—non-alcoholic is fine, too, if that is your preference
- some volume measures—jiggers for spirits and cups for other ingredients
- a variety of glasses
- a cocktail shaker
- a cocktail strainer
- a blender
- a stirrer
- ice
- a variety of garnishes—strawberries, orange slices, olives
- kitchen towels for any spills

Date Instructions

You can use the drink recipes in this book as a starting point but don't be afraid to try other cocktails.

Once you are comfortable making some drinks recipes, start experimenting with ingredients to invent drinks you think your partner would like. Take turns creating a new drink for each other.

You can also withhold the list of ingredients from each other and play a game to have the taster guess the contents of their glass. Or, you can choose two elements each and challenge your partner to create a drink including those ingredients.

DATE NUMBER 6: ABC DATE

This date idea allows you and your partner to let loose and go with your creative flow for the night. It can be done at home or out and about for the evening. It all depends on your available budget that week. Because it is a flexible date night, There is no list of suggested equipment. However, keep a notepad to write your goals and scores.

Date Instructions

You can do this date more than once and take turns to be the chooser, or choose the below points together before you start:

- Choose a letter of the alphabet.
- Choose a number between one and nine.
- Choose a color theme.

1. You and your partner should come to the date wearing an outfit representing the letter, number, and color theme you chose.

2. When you go out on your date, you should include your chosen letter, number, and color as often as possible. For example, the name of your restaurant could start with your desired letter, your letter could be in the street name of a park you visit, or you can use ingredients that begin with your letter if you are cooking at home.

3. Award yourselves points for every time you include your chosen letter, number, or color, counting two points for every time the color is present and one point for each time you have your desired letter or number.

4. At the end of your date, add up your score and give yourselves a rating:

- 20 points: Congratulations, you had a solid date
- 15–19 points: It wasn't perfect, but you had a reasonable date.
- 10–14 points: You made a good effort and had fun.
- Less than 10 points: Have fun trying again!

DATE NUMBER 7: MENU CREATION

This date hits two birds with one stone—it takes some stress out of choosing what to cook every day by planning and challenges you and your partner to spend time together problem-solving with your creativity. The aim is to create your menu for the whole week together; you can start with the recipes included in this book or use some popular family favorites in your home.

Suggested Equipment

- a calendar to block out each day's meal plan
- a calculator to help budget
- a notepad to record any ingredients that you need to buy for each recipe
- a recipe book if you have a favorite that you like to follow

Date Instructions

First, set a budget for your weekly menu. Let's say $250 is a good weekly spend for four family members, plus $25 for each additional person in your home. However, you could also budget per person. Below is an *example* of how you can calculate your budget:

1. 3 meals x 7 days = 21 meals $--- per meal x 21 meals= $----

2. 2 snacks x 7 days = 14 snacks $--- per snack x 14 snacks = $---

3. Add the final amount from lines one and two for an estimated budget.

Once you have a budget, plan which meals you would like on the calendar and list all the ingredients you need to buy. Be sure to go the extra mile and have each other's favorite meals at least once a week. Remember, sometimes doing life together is the best date night idea!

DATE NUMBER 8: IMAGINARY WEDDING

Have fun with this activity, whether you are planning to get married or are already married. The goal is to explore what your ideal wedding would look like if money were no object. Think about each other's tastes and have fun choosing things that you think each other would love to see. Consider the following for your imaginary wedding plan:

- You don't have a budget.
- You have no restrictions on the location you choose.

- You can choose any date, time, and season.
- All your guests will be able to attend regardless of your choice; it's your imagination. You can invite celebrities and idols to share your special day, too.

Ask Yourself:

- Who will officiate for you?
- Where will the honeymoon be?
- What would your color theme be?
- What would be your dream dress or suit?
- Who will sing at the wedding?
- What food would you serve?
- What would your dress code be?

Enjoy an unlimited imagination date, have fun and break any rules in planning your wedding.

DATE NUMBER 9: MEMORY LANE

This date night is about reminding yourself how many precious memories you have made and sharing a night of reminiscing with each other.

Suggested Equipment

- printed or developed photographs
- a library of digital photographs

Date Instructions

1. Gather your photographs together and try to choose a variety of occasions and time frames.

2. Go through your photographs and discuss your event memories with each other. Remember the following:

- When was the picture taken, and where was it?
- Who is in the photo?
- What was the occasion?
- Is it good quality?
- Do you like it enough to want to add it to a physical or virtual album?

If you choose to put it in an album, record the date and location before filing it away.

DATE NUMBER 10: SECRET CODE

Using nicknames may seem cheesy, but having a unique language for you and your partner can increase relationship satisfaction, encouraging you to be more playful and resilient. There isn't a specific list of suggested equipment for this date. Maybe a notepad and a pen to record your ideas.

Date Instructions

Create your language for letting each other know you are thinking of them and they are loved. Think of alternative ways to say the following things:

- I love you, e.g., You are incredible.
- I can't wait to go home with you, e.g., Home is waiting for us.
- I wish we were alone, e.g., Two's company, three's a crowd.
- I love how you look tonight, e.g., Eat your heart out, Fred Astaire.
- I am glad you are my guy/gal –e.g., You're my person.

Create your code for discussing money. Think of alternative ways to say the following things:

- We can't afford that right now, e.g., Let's add it to the list for next month.
- Let's split the tab with the other couple, e.g., Shall we half?
- Use your credit card, e.g., Use plastic.

You can also experiment with swapping out vowels in written messages to each other or substitute letters for symbols.

MOVING ON...

Now that you have practiced getting creative together let's dial up the adventure factor in the next chapter, with the adventure dates 11 to 20.

4

THE ADVENTUROUS ACTIVITIES

Sharing adventures with your partner can uncover more about one another. One couple, Ryan Fontana and Molly Joseph, learned the meaning of love while they adventured around the world, living their lives to the fullest and discovering the world together. The couple quit their jobs and sold all of their belongings to enable them to pursue the adventure and gain a new perspective while at it. They recorded their travels on their Instagram accounts. At the end of it all, they shared the lessons they learned along the way.

> *Sharing ourselves completely with our partner, we begin to shine light into all of the areas of ourselves that we have shrouded in darkness, making the seemingly unlovable lovable once more. This is what it means to love unconditionally.* –Ryan Fontana

> *It's crazy to think that only three years ago I was a cancer patient, seeing doctor after doctor in New York. When I think of where I've been in comparison to where I am now, I know for sure that anything is possible and that dreams do come true. I know that hitting the bottom makes life at the top that much sweeter, that without the lows, the highs would be meaningless.* –Molly Joseph

Ryan and Molly's story included an enormous change in their lifestyles, but if you don't want to make such a dramatic change, you can still bring the spirit of adventure into your lives with the date nights featured in this chapter.

DATE NUMBER 11: RANDOM CARDS

This date encourages you and your partner to trust one another, choose activities you will enjoy, and follow through if you are drawing out the cards. Using this date idea, you can be as adventurous as you dare.

Suggested Equipment

- cards—make your own or use pre-made note cards
- pens

Date Instructions

1. Take five cards each and write out a different act on each card. Choose five actions for your partner that they must perform for you.

2. Take turns picking a card and doing whatever is on it.

3. Depending on the time of day, you can choose to perform the act on the card immediately or save it for later—you can even save it for your next date night, but you must follow through.

Some examples you can use on your cards are:

- Tell me that you love me in ten languages—you can Google them if you don't know ten!
- Read a love poem to me.
- Write a poem for me.

DATE NUMBER 12: CHOOSE A DESTINATION

This date aims for you and your partner to share the excitement of discovering new things together. There are no set items needed since you can either travel in person or take a virtual tour, but if you choose a virtual tour, use a device that has a high screen resolution so you can enjoy photographs of the area to their fullest.

Date Instructions

1. Choose a place together, one that you are both interested in but have yet to be there.

2. If you can travel, book it together and have fun choosing your itinerary. If you are going on a virtual tour, sit together in a comfortable place where you can enjoy your internet adventure.

3. Consider learning about the following:

- the local food
- the history
- the local language
- the culture
- traditional activities enjoyed in the area

DATE NUMBER 13: VIRTUAL CONCERT

This date brings the excitement of the music stage to your own home. There isn't any set equipment needed, but a good-quality screen and speakers are worth using if you have them.

Date Instructions

1. Choose a concert you both want to see and can access via streaming service, DVD, or online. It doesn't have to be a new concert; if you have an old favorite that you both love to revisit, that is a great choice too.

2. Get together to watch the concert, make an effort to make the room comfortable, and dress as you would if you attended it in person. This will add a sense of a special occasion to your date.

3. You can look up some lyrics and sing them together.

DATE NUMBER 14: PARTNER'S CHOICE

This date forces you to trust your partner, who will have 100% control over the date. It teaches you to let go of the reins and trust them to take you in a direction that will be great for both of you. As the date will be entirely in your partner's control, There is no defined list of suggested equipment.

Date Instructions

Choose a day for your date one week ahead and give your partner full authority to plan it—let them choose to be adventurous and surprise you. Try to avoid asking them questions about the date ahead of time, as the anticipation of discovering the secret plans will make a date more exciting.

There is only one unbreakable rule: If you are the date planner this time around, do not make your partner do anything that would make them uncomfortable. The goal is to have fun!

DATE NUMBER 15: WILD CARDS

Sometimes, it may not be challenging to voice the things you love to do for your partner, or you forget running a household can be taxing if one person does more than the other. This is your chance to give your partner some time as a gift. Express your gratitude to them.

Suggested Equipment

- 20 index cards/small gift tags
- a variety of pens
- other items as needed

Date Instructions

1. Decide on the acts you would commit to at the start of your date.

2. Discuss your boundaries and learn what you are happy to offer and what they would value getting from you.

3. Split your index cards into groups of five.

4. Write five chores you promise to do for your partner on the first group of cards. Here are a few examples:

- Cook a meal from scratch.
- Do the school runs every day this week.
- Handle the grocery shopping.

5. On the next group of cards, write five different acts of intimacy that you promise to do for your partner. Some examples could include the following:

- one hour of hugging while watching a movie of their choice
- learning to style their hair for them
- promising to text every day at lunchtime to ask about their day

6. On five cards, write the words "Free Time For One Hour." With these cards, you promise to give your partner one hour of your time without distractions.

7. On the final five cards, write the words "WILD CARD." With these cards, you promise to allow your partner to choose another card or allocate an act they would like you to perform. Remember, if you are the giftee, don't choose anything that will make your partner uncomfortable.

8. Shuffle the cards together and allow your partner to choose a random card. Depending on the task written on the selected card, it can be gifted immediately or kept more appropriately at your partner's agreement.

9. You can continue drawing cards immediately and stack them up in order, or you save the rest of the cards and allow your partner to draw one daily for the next 19 days.

DATE NUMBER 16: CYBER DATE

This date is about getting to know one another more deeply. By understanding each other more, we can learn how to be more attentive to each other in our everyday lives.

Suggested Equipment

- a stable connection to the internet
- notepad
- pens

Date Instructions

Use online personality tests to get to know yourselves and each other better. Start with one of the following quizzes:

1. The 16 personalities Myers-Briggs test. This quiz is about 15 minutes each. It will break down five groupings of your character and access which end of the scale you fall for the following pairs. It then allocates a five-letter acronym from the first letter of each type that you display:

- Mind: Are you introverted or extroverted?
- Energy: Are you observant or intuitive?
- Nature: Are you thinking or feeling?

- Tactics: Are you judging or prospecting?
- Identity: Are you assertive or turbulent?

Following this, your acronym will also then determine your role category. The roles help you understand how your behavior fits into the broader world. These roles are:

- Analysts: INTJ-A/T, INTP-A/T, ENTJ-A/T, ENTP-A/T
- Diplomats: INFJ-A/T, INFP-A/T, ENFJ-A/T, ENFP-A/T
- Sentinels: ISTJ-A/T, ISFJ-A/T, ESTJ-A/T, ESFJ-A/T
- Explorers: ISTP-A/T, ISFP-A/T, ESTP-A/T, ESFP-A/T

Spend time together learning about your personality types and have fun exploring how much you agree or disagree that the assessments match each of you. The quiz will also familiarize you more with your partner's outlook on life if they have struggled to verbalize it before or vice versa.

2. A very similar test to the 16 personalities quiz is the Nanaya test. Although based on the Myers-Briggs acronym system, the role analysis focuses more on how

you approach romantic relationships rather than a general life perspective.

3. Take a love language quiz; these tests teach you how each of you prefers to have love expressed towards you. There are five types of love languages—your results can be a mixture of each style. Still, it will help you to understand if you have been giving each other the wrong kinds of signals in affection and how to fix this.

- Acts of service: You like to get help around the house and expect your partner to follow through when they make promises to complete tasks for you.
- Quality time: You feel most loved when your partner chooses to spend time alone, share a hobby, or experience something new together.
- Physical touch: You like to have physical contact with your partner throughout the day; holding hands, hugging, and kissing are essential, and you worry if it happens less than usual.
- Words of affirmation: You feel most loved when your partner expresses how much they value you. Getting praise and having them remind you that they are proud of you often will give you a warm fuzzy feeling.

- Receiving gifts: You feel loved when your partner thinks of you while you are apart and brings you a present when they return to show you how they felt. Gifts don't have to be a grand gesture either—something as small as receiving a handwritten love note in a packed lunch can make you smile.

4. Another option is creating your quizzes for one another. Think along the lines of the "Newlywed" game, where you both answer the same question about yourselves and each other, then compare your responses. Here are some example questions:

- What is your partner's favorite clothing color?
- Who are their best or closest friends?
- Where is their favorite place to eat?
- What is the biggest worry they have?
- What is one food they will never try?
- What is your partner's dream?
- How many children do they want?
- What is their philosophy of life?
- What is their favorite sport to watch or play?
- What is your partner's biggest pet peeve?
- Who is their favorite family member?
- What kind of car would they like to drive?

DATE NUMBER 17: PARK DATE

This date aims to rekindle your sense of adventure and play. The aim is to have fun and get in touch with your inner kid. There is no suggested equipment for this date.

Date Instructions

1. You can choose a local park for a few hours or take a whole day trip and head to a tourist park or city gardens further away from home. If you have children and want to include them on some of your dates, this is the perfect one to take them along on. However, ensure that the day doesn't become solely about the kids—you and your partner should be enjoying it too.

2. Enjoy some time playing on the swings, using the slides, or having a game of mini-golf if there is one available. The idea is to make the most of the park's equipment to let loose and do things you usually wouldn't.

3. Afterward, go for some ice cream, get some street food, and sit down to talk. The goal of this park date is to enjoy your time together.

DATE NUMBER 18: SCAVENGER HUNT

This date will trigger your curiosity. It is about you and your partner learning more about your local area while exploring together and spending time cooperating. No specific equipment is needed, but you will want to take a checklist to tick off your itinerary items as you find them.

Date Instructions

Cooperate to find and do all of the items on the scavenger hunt list. Be sure to take photographs when you see them as evidence that you didn't skip anything on the list and as a sweet memento for the two of you to look back on together. You can search as near home or as far away as your budget for the date allows. If it is further than walking distance, consider using public transport instead of driving, so you can enjoy each other rather than concentrate on the road.

Scavenger Hunt Checklist

- Find a cafe/restaurant, the name of which begins with the letter H.
- Look for blue flowers.
- Buy a newspaper or magazine.
- Speak to a street food/food truck vendor.
- Walk over a bridge.

- Ask to pet someone's dog.
- Find a red house.
- Look for a green car.
- Stand beneath a stop sign.
- Visit a street, the name of which begins with the letter L.
- Eat ice cream.
- Sit beneath an evergreen tree.
- Find a black door.
- Talk to a public service worker.
- Rest on a park bench.
- Find some ducks.
- Look for a retail store, the name of which begins with the letter M.
- Find a building with the number 32 in the address.
- Buy some candy/chocolate.
- Visit a museum.

DATE NUMBER 19: PLANT TOGETHER

Relationships are often likened to caring for a plant—if it is tended, watered regularly, and given enough light, it will flourish and grow. However, if neglected, it withers and dies. This date brings the metaphor to life and encourages you both to look after the plant; it will be easier and more rewarding if you share the work of tending to its needs.

Suggested Equipment

- seeds/bulbs/seedlings of herbs, flowers, or succulents
- drainage medium/loose gravel
- soil/compost
- seedling pot and a larger pot to transfer the plant into as it grows
- watering can or a cup you can use to water the plant
- plant food

Date Instructions

1. Cooperate, taking turns to complete each step of planting and nurturing the plant as it grows later.

2. Place your drainage medium in the bottom of your plant pot.

3. Fill ⅔ the pot with soil/compost.

4. Place your seed/bulb/seedling on top of the soil in the center.

5. If you have a seed or bulb, cover it with soil, adding more until the solid level reaches about ½ inch away

from the top of the pot. If you have a seedling, fill in the dirt around the root ball and avoid covering the young plant with soil. Compress the solid around the seedling gently with your fingers.

6. Water the pot generously, and if you have a seedling, add plant food as guided by the instructions on the box/bottle.

7. Be sure to research the needs of your chosen plant and feed/water appropriately for its type.

8. Continue to care for the plant weekly and share the work of watering, weeding, and feeding it. Enjoy the reward of seeing it grow and its beautiful blossoms if your chosen plant is a flowering variety.

DATE NUMBER 20: THE LONG WALK

This date aims to increase your attention to detail by practicing noticing things that you wouldn't usually see while you are focused on your daily tasks. It will help you notice subtle changes in your partner's behavior or your relationship as a whole so that you can better respond to the identified needs. The date is an opportunity for you to relax together. There is no specific equipment needed for this date.

Date Instructions

1. Plan a walk together that includes a lot of beautiful scenery. Think about where your favorite places are in the town/city area and your favorite nature spots.

2. Include along your route where you can stop to buy a coffee or any drink of preference. Consider looking at seasonal drink menus to try something new together.

3. Take your drinks to an outdoor seating area or a park bench. Use this as an opportunity to relax together; you can do some soft breathing together or deep tummy breathing exercises to encourage a feeling of calm.

4. If your chosen rest spot is somewhere busy, use it as an opportunity to people-watch. See if you can guess their stories and compare your ideas about the people passing by.

5. If your chosen rest spot is in a quiet location, then use the time to look around for signs of nature that you wouldn't usually notice. Are there flowers you haven't seen, or is there a pleasant smell of cut grass? Point out the things you notice to each other and enjoy the scenery.

6. Once you have finished your drinks, you can return home or continue your walk to discover more about your locality.

MOVING ON...

Now you have had the opportunity to wake up your creative sides and culture a sense of adventure together. It is time to think about building intimacy. Relationships are built around our emotional connection to one another and require familiarity to foster that connection. In the next chapter, you will be guided through ten date nights that will encourage the magic of your emotional side to show through and rekindle your passion for each other through intimacy.

5

THE PERSONAL ACTIVITIES

To improve intimacy in your relationship, think of it as a living thing that changes throughout your life. As you mature, your and your partner's needs change, so be open to that and acknowledge it in your relationship. –Graeme Orr

Intimacy comes in two forms: physical and emotional. For a relationship to remain healthy, it needs to have a balance of both types; too much physical intimacy without emotional backup can lead to distrust, while too much emotional intimacy and a lack of physical connection can lead to decreased self-confidence.

Intimacy is a basic human need to connect with those we love. As it changes form along the course of our relationships, it is essential to keep nurturing our physical and emotional intimacy to keep our connection solid and fulfilling.

DATE NUMBER 21: ALTERNATIVE ENDING

Practice telling each other the reasons behind your decisions or the emotional input into your ideals.

Suggested Equipment

- TV or other devices that you can stream a movie onto
- streaming service, cable, or DVD to watch a movie
- two notepads or index cards
- pens

Date Instructions

1. Choose a movie together that you are familiar with but love to watch again. The chosen movie needs to be one you enjoy; if you settle for one that isn't your preference, then the date exercise will be redundant as you won't engage in the story.

2. Before you start watching the movie, both partners should write on their own notepad/index card an alternative ending that suits the characters or storyline. Only show each other your rewritten endings once the movie has finished.

3. After the movie ends, show each other your alternative endings.

4. Spend time discussing why you chose the ending that you did. What is it about your movie ending that you think is significant? What do you think about how you and your partner view similar situations?

DATE NUMBER 22: POPCORN AND ROMANCE

This date aims to rekindle the romance. You can get inspiration from the movies you choose to watch and enjoy a peaceful time with your partner.

Suggested Equipment

- a TV or other device that you can stream a movie onto
- a streaming service, cable, or DVD to watch a movie
- candles
- blankets and pillows
- popcorn and other snacks

Date Instructions

1. Ask your partner to list their top five favorite romantic movies.

2. Choose one to watch without revealing to your partner which one you have chosen.

3. Have a home-cooked dinner or take-out at the beginning of your date.

4. After dinner, light some candles, dim the light, and cozy up on the couch with plenty of blankets and pillows. Don't forget the popcorn or your other favorite snacks.

5. Watch the movie together and enjoy the atmosphere in your romantic setting.

6. At the end of the night, you can discuss the movie and rate it out of ten together.

DATE NUMBER 23: LOVELY ADJECTIVES

This date encourages you to give each other kind words of affirmation. It will help you to express the things you love about one another. No specific equipment is needed for this date; however, this book includes a list of positive adjectives.

Date Instructions

1. Make dinner together, or order takeout.

2. Over dinner, share your words of affirmation and discuss why you think those words apply to each other. Discussing anything that makes you proud of each other is especially helpful.

3. Ask each other if there are other words that they think apply to you or any that they appreciate about you. Then do the same for them, explaining any other expressions you want to give them. If either of you needs some more ideas, you can refer to the list of example adjectives at the back of the book.

4. After dinner, use the things you have discussed to write a list of five affirmations for your partner and ask them to do the same for you. Examples of positive affirmations include:

- You are a caring and sensitive partner and love our children unconditionally.
- You are a strong and confident person capable of great things.
- You are a good person and show kindness every day.
- You are beautiful/handsome and deserve the compliments that you receive.

- You are an intelligent person who can achieve all of your goals.

5. Exchange the written lists with each other and place them somewhere prominent in your home where you can see them daily. Good locations include the vanity mirror, the bathroom mirror, a PC monitor if you use it daily, the bedside alarm, or a lamp.

DATE NUMBER 24: HAPPY MEDIUM

This date aims to remind you that compromise is good. You are not alone, and there is always a way to reach a happy medium with your partner. It will help you recognize how much you love each other when you can choose options that suit you both.

Suggested Equipment

- two notepads
- two pens

Date Instructions

1. On a piece of paper, you should write down the names of ten of your favorite movies.

2. Swap your papers and rate each with a score from one to ten on how willing you would be to watch that

movie with your partner. Number one would be the most likely that you would watch it together, and number ten being the least likely.

3. Use your lists to find the happy medium, the movie you both agree you would be willing to watch together. Are there any movies on both of your lists? Which movies had the best rating from both of you?

4. You can repeat this list rating process for several things you would like to do together. Other examples include:

- foods to eat
- sports to play/watch
- activities you want to try
- sleeping styles
- cooking activities
- shopping destinations
- places to travel to
- people to visit
- favorite animals

DATE NUMBER 25: A NEW LIFE

This date aims to be fun and creative while allowing you to express how you view the things in your life.

There is no specific equipment needed as this date is conversational.

Date Instructions

1. Get together and review everyone in your life—all the people you see daily or who are important to you.

2. Come up with new names for all of those people. Choose terms that suit their characters or roles if you aren't close enough to know them well. You don't have to choose serious names; you can have fun using cartoon characters or real-life celebrity's names. You could also use flowers, colors, or months for inspiration.

3. Compare the list of names you have chosen with your partner's. Discuss why you chose each name, what things you associate with that person, and what name you chose for them. Did either of you pick the exact words for anyone? If you did, were your reasons the same? Have fun discussing your newly imagined characters; keep it light-toned, and remember that the objective isn't to denounce anyone you dislike.

DATE NUMBER 26: IMAGINE THAT

If you could rewrite your life, how would it be? This date focuses on reimagining your own story and that of your partner. It's a chance to explore your dreams and share some ambitions. The equipment needed for this date will vary greatly depending on what you choose to change about your life.

Date Instructions

1. Please share any ideas about your story with your partner as you rewrite it, and listen to their opinions. Consider the following aspects:

- Where would you be born?
- What language would you speak?
- What era is it?
- Would you have a different job?
- Would you have studied in the same field?

2. Once you have both dreamed up a new story for yourselves, use the information that night for an impromptu role-play.

3. You can also save the ideas for a future date, giving you time to prepare for each other's ideas.

4. If you decide to keep the information for another date, use all the information you decided on to set the scene for your date. This activity can have a budget as large or as small as you like—it doesn't need to break the bank to still have fun with it. For example, if you

choose Germany as your birthplace, then cook some German food and listen to some German music. Born in a different era would change the clothing you wear and dress for your date using that inspiration.

DATE NUMBER 27: THE LOVE STORY

Your love story is unique to you; no one will have experienced their story the same way. You might both have impeccable memories right now, but this may only sometimes be the case, and sometime during disagreements, you may forget what brought you together in the first place. Writing it all down can help us remember why we love each other.

This date is a record-keeping exercise, but the rewards are much more significant than just having a written account of your story. Like in *The Notebook*, you will get a physical memento of your time together and a record to remind you of how it all began and how far you have come since then. The date will allow you to spend quality time with your partner, reminiscing about your relationship and having a unique chance to hear the story from their perspective. In the future, your tale could become a beautiful keepsake for your grandchildren.

Suggested Equipment

- notepad
- pen
- tablet or laptop for digital recording

Date Instructions

Spend your date reminiscing about the story of your relationship. It doesn't matter if you have been together for one year or 40 years—looking back at the things you two have been through will be just as valuable.

Write down all of the things you can recall about your story; think about the following details:

1. When was the first time you saw one another?
2. What were your first impressions?
3. Why were you at that place?
4. Who introduced you?
5. What attracted you to one another?
6. When was your first date?
7. What did you wear?
8. How did you feel?
9. Whom did you tell about it?
10. Did you wait to call/message each other?
11. When did you meet each other's family?
12. What was your first holiday together?

13. How soon did you know that your partner was the right person for you?
14. What made you think you wanted to spend the rest of your life with them?
15. Were there any barriers to you getting together?

DATE NUMBER 28: QUIET DATE

If you have ever said, "we are going to have a quiet Date Night at home. This activity challenges you to test your emotional intimacy with your partner by communicating without speaking. You will have to rely on the subtle signals you may already give each other every day and not notice; it will also help you develop more emotional cues to understand each other.

Suggested Equipment

- Kitchen utensils
- ingredients needed to cook a dinner of your choice
- a device you can use to play music
- candles

Date Instructions

1. Plan for your date to be a quiet evening with no distractions from anyone else.

2. Quiet doesn't mean peace from the outside world either—the two of you must spend the evening without speaking to each other, and all communication must be some other way. Please consider banning your phones from the room, too.

3. Prepare your meal with no noise other than the cooking sounds.Turn off your lights and light candles when you sit to eat your meal. You can put on some low-volume calm or romantic music too.

4. Use your senses to enjoy the date. Hold each other often and make small, extra efforts, like pulling out a chair for your partner and pouring their wine for them.

5. Once you have eaten, use the music to dance together. You can even imagine your music and dance in silence together if you prefer.

DATE NUMBER 29: BUCKET LIST

This date is about expression and working collaboratively to achieve your goals. The wonderful thing about a joint bucket list is that you will put effort into completing the activities on your checklist. The date will foster a sense of support for one another and light a spark for adventure. Depending on how far along you are in your relationship, you should set larger or smaller goals accordingly. You may have already experienced many things that you want to share.

Suggested Equipment

- pen
- notepad
- tablet

Date Instructions

Spend some time creating a bucket list. Consider what you would like to achieve this year, where you would like to be in the next five or ten years, and what you would like to experience together during those time frames.

Remember, your bucket list reflects you; you can change your mind about things as you go along and replace items or goals if you have decided they are no longer relevant to you.

Here are some examples of questions that you may want to consider while creating your list together:

1. Where do you each want to be with your studies/career by the end of this year?

2. Do you want to live in the same place you do now in the next five years?

3. Do you see yourselves having children, or more children, in the next five years?

4. Do you see yourselves wanting to get pets, or more pets, in the next five years?

5. Is there anywhere that either of you wants to visit this year?

6. Do you want to try any new activities or hobbies this month?

DATE NUMBER 30: THE SPA DATE

This date gives you an opportunity to practice your physical intimacy as well as your emotional intimacy. You can pamper each other and enjoy time relaxing together.

Suggested Equipment

- bath robes
- slippers
- purchased face masks or ingredients to make your own
- bath bombs or bubble bath

- other spa kit items such as body lotion, hand cream, etc.
- candles

Date Instructions

1. Get together and watch a few tutorials on YouTube about making and applying spa products. Also, look for tutorials that will teach you how to give each other a massage.

2. Light some candles and play some relaxing music in the bathroom.

3. Draw a warm bath using a bath bomb or bubble bath. If your bath allows you to, share one; if not, take it in turns. While waiting for your partner, you can consider reading their favorite book or mixing the ingredients for each other's face mask.

4. After your baths, wrap up warm in your bath robes and slippers, then apply each other's face masks. Keep the lights dimmed, and candles lit for ultimate relaxation; you can also consider using aromatherapy candles.

5. Once the masks have been on for the recommended time, wash them away and moisturize your face.

6. Now, you should be feeling fresh; experiment with giving each other a massage using the tutorials that you found online.

7. Finish your spa treatments by treating each other to a hand massage using hand and nail cream.

8. If you want to dial the date up a notch, you can emulate the food you find in a professional spa, such as afternoon tea and prosecco.

DATE NUMBER 31: DREAM BOARD

The dream board is similar to a bucket list but more practical, containing a visualization of goals you want to achieve—an excellent place to list your big dreams and how you will reach them together.

Suggested Equipment

- a cork notice board or a paper a-frame board
- magazines or tourist brochures that you can take images from
- a variety of pens and paper types
- if you wish to compile your dream board online, you will need a suitable tablet or laptop to design it on

Date Instructions

Think of the dreams that you both have and pick out some that you can both work together to achieve. When choosing the goals you want to include on your board, consider the following questions:

- Where do you see your relationship/marriage in five years?
- How do you see your finances growing in the next five years?
- What will your careers look like in five years?
- Will you have children in the next five years? What will their needs be?
- Where do you want to travel together?
- What do you each want to learn?
- Is there a significant purchase you want, such as a house or car?
- Do you have any aspirations for schooling?
- Do you like to know any languages?

When making your board together, don't just list the dreams you have agreed to accomplish. Make the board exciting to look at and something that is fun to return to and renew when things change.

Add pictures to your board to visualize your dreams. For example, if you want to buy a house, add a photograph of one similar to what you want. If you travel, add a picture of your ultimate destination, beach, or cityscape. If you're going to study, add the logo of the college you want to attend.

If your dream board is exciting and inviting to you, you will be more likely to look at it often, reinforcing your goals each time you do. Consider adding a progress bar if you are saving money to travel or a scorecard for grades if you hope to get into a college.

MOVING ON...

You now have experience in practicing both emotional and physical intimacy together. You have created a strong foundation for your relationship in your creativity, adventure, and personal activity date nights. Now it is time to have some fun! The next chapter is all about getting playful together.

6

THE PLAYFUL ACTIVITIES

Setting up date nights centered around playful activities is a great way to bring out and nurture your inner child. Having an inner child can be challenging for some people to connect with; if you feel this way, you can approach it as a way to relate to your past experiences rather than an actual child version of yourself.

Keeping a healthy relationship with your inner child and understanding your unique pattern of development in the past can increase your understanding of your adult relationships and help you find joy in everyday small things. Consider involving children in date night activities if you have children. Their responses to the games and ideas will be a great source of learning for you and your partner to live more in the moment.

DATE NUMBER 32: MYSTERY TASTE-TESTING

This date adds a sense of wonder to your time together. It encourages you to see things for what they are rather than accepting they should be a certain way based on a label. In turn, this will help you allow yourselves more freedom and natural flow in your relationship rather than putting yourself into a corner based on the label you assume you should take.

Suggested Equipment

- a variety of beverages in cans—alcoholic drinks are acceptable to be included if you feel it is appropriate
- duct tape

Date Instructions

1. Gather your selected drinks and cover the names and any recognizable branding or colors on the can with duct tape.

2. Taste-test each drink and see if you can guess what is inside each can. Once you have guessed, you can peel back the tape to see how many of you guessed correctly. You can have a competition to see who scores the highest.

3. Repeat this with other food or drink, or make the date night last longer by including a few different kinds at once. Some examples of food that is great for this activity include:

- bags of chips
- packets of candy—be sure to avoid brands that include their name on the candy itself or have a distinctive shape
- wine bottles
- soda bottles—avoid brands with uniquely shaped bottles

DATE NUMBER 33: TOTAL STRANGER

This date whisks you back to the start of your relationship and allows you to remember all the little details that first attracted you to one another. It will enable you to use your imagination and have fun pretending to meet each other for the first time. No specific equipment for this date; consider choosing a bar or restaurant you haven't visited before to help create a sense of the date being a first-time experience.

Date Instructions

1. Pretend that the two of you have never met before. Imagine that this is the first date set up for the two of you by a mutual friend.

2. You should both get ready for your date in different rooms so that you won't see each other for a short time before the date begins. Doing this will help you feel the excitement of the moment you are revealed to each other on and build an atmosphere for a special occasion.

3. It helps you stay immersed in your fantasy first date if you each arrive at the bar separately. If it isn't an option, having an exciting reveal in your living room or hallway is fine if you live together. Wherever you meet for the first time that evening, be sure to introduce yourselves as you would at the beginning of any other first date.

4. Use an icebreaker conversation that includes details about your mutual friend; then, you can move on to getting to know each other. Offer to buy a drink for your new date.

5. Consider asking each other the questions below; it can be easy to assume that you already know these answers, but you would be surprised how often we forget these details about one another over time:

- Where were you born?
- What do you do for work/study?
- What do you like to eat/drink?
- What is your favorite color?
- What music do you like?
- Do you enjoy reading?/Who is your favorite author?
- What is your favorite animal?
- What would be your dream future?

6. Ask your date if they would like to dance.

7. Offer to give your date a ride home or to walk them home.

DATE NUMBER 34: GAME NIGHT

This date will draw out your playful sides. For some, playing games might be a bit daunting or silly, but it is a great way to nurture your ability to enjoy the moment and have fun without feeling unproductive with your time.

Suggested Equipment

Ideally, choose the game ahead of your date so you can get the necessary items for it; however, if you want to go with the flow, then the below equipment will be helpful:

- a selection of board games
- a deck of cards
- a suitable table to play on—dining tables are a great option

Date Instructions

1. Option one is to find your partner's favorite game ahead of time.

2. Option two is to look for a game neither of you has played before so you can learn it together, purchasing the game ahead of time.

3. Option three is to gather a selection of games you may already have or can borrow from friends and pick a game randomly on your date. You may even want to play more than one game.

Whichever option you choose to go with, the main rule is that you both have fun learning or following the guidelines for the game. Remember, it doesn't have to be a board game. If the two of you enjoy using game consoles, that's a great idea, too—be sure to choose games you can both play. Here are some game suggestions if you aren't familiar with them:

Board Games

- Monopoly
- Chess
- Risk
- Quacks of Quedlinburg

Card Games

- Slap
- Go Fish
- Blackjack
- Gin Rummy
- Hearts
- Uno
- Magic The Gathering
- Apples to Apples

Console Games

- Army of Two
- Call of Duty
- Lego, Star Wars/Batman, etc.
- Halo
- It Takes Two

DATE NUMBER 35: STATE THE STATES

This date will encourage you to explore a sense of make-believe. This game will be the most fun if you are willing to embrace any outrageous ideas you have during the game.

Suggested Equipment

- a printed map of the U.S.A.
- various pens

Date Instructions

1. Print yourselves a copy of the American state map.

2. Blank out the current state names. You can do this digitally before you print your map or cover the text with correction fluid or tape.

3. You two are in charge of assigning a name to each state. Be creative and choose new words that make you smile, inspire, or remind you of the state. For each state, you could consider using the following ideas for names:

- numbers
- colors
- fruits
- baby names
- movie titles

4. Remember your new names for as long as possible; you can have an inside joke between the two of you by referring to your imagined state names in conversation.

5. Play this game as often as you like, with minor changes to keep it fresh and fun. You could set a theme the next time you play and try to name all states after things within your theme, for example:

- all flowers
- all girl names
- all animals

6. Next time you play, consider marking the states you have visited and those you would like to see.

DATE NUMBER 36: THE BOOK DATE

This date creates a space for you to spend quality time with your partner, where you can share the experience of hearing a story or learning new facts together. The familiarity of your partner's voice is something that you may take for granted, but this date will help you strengthen your emotional bond and gain a new admiration for each other when you hear your voice.

Suggested Equipment

- a variety of books to choose from
- a device to read a digital book if preferred
- snacks and drinks

Date Instructions

1. Discuss your favorite books or books you would like to read and choose one to use for this date. It doesn't necessarily need to be a novel—short stories, poetry, and non-fiction books are also okay if it suits your tastes.

2. Settle down in a room where you can be comfortable and undisturbed. Bring snacks and drinks, and put some quiet music on in the background if you are uncomfortable with no background sound.

3. Take turns reading a page or a chapter aloud to one another. Have fun trying out different voices, reading sections as if they are poems, or even singing parts.

4. Discuss the content of your chosen book once you have finished reading. You can think of the following questions to help your discussion:

- Does it motivate you?
- Does it resonate with your emotions?
- What did it mean to you?
- Could it encourage you to change your future?
- Did you learn anything?

DATE NUMBER 37: FANTASY GAME

This date encourages you to play with the idea of having an alternative life. You can imagine who your ideal family would be if you could choose anyone in the world to fill those spots. It will help you and your partner learn more about how each of you interacts with other people in a light and fun way. No specific equipment is needed, but you may note the fantasy lives you built together so you can look back on them again.

Date Instructions

1. During this date, the two of you will retain your current identities. The only changes will be to the people who surround you. Create a fantasy world around you while you enjoy the evening together. Have discussions with each other during the evening as if the things you have chosen are natural for you.

2. Choose who the people around you would be in your fantasy life. You can choose celebrities, TV or novel characters, or other people you admire. Be as imagina-

tive as possible, and keep it upbeat—the more fun or entertaining your fantasy world is, the better. Consider who would be the following people:

- your mother or father
- your partner's mother or father
- your siblings
- your children
- your best friends

DATE NUMBER 38: SILENT MOVIE DATE

This activity allows you and your partner to be as silly or creative as you dare together. The intention is that you spend the date creating as much laughter as possible, strengthening your emotional bond, and alleviating any stress either of you may be feeling.

Suggested Equipment

- a selection of movies
- an appropriate device to play your film on that has a mute function
- popcorn, nachos, or other cinema favorite snacks
- plenty of pillows and blankets to get comfortable in

Date Instructions

1. Choose a movie to watch together, get comfortable with blanks and pillows, and set your movie to play on mute.

2. While the movie plays with no sound, have fun making your lines or the sounds around the characters.

3. Come up with an alternative dialogue, or guess the actors' lines. Go wild using funny voices or pretending to be background sounds.

4. An alternative to this date is to play the movie in a different language and try translating.

DATE NUMBER 39: PUZZLE DATE

This date night gives you something to focus on together, giving you a sense of achievement when it is all done. The satisfaction of having finished it together will boost your admiration for one another. Also, consider that you are a piece of a more significant puzzle. Alone you are just a collection of parts, but together you create a beautiful picture of your lives—an image that can be valued and admired.

Suggested Equipment

- a picture puzzle of your choice
- a suitable surface to work on together. A dining or coffee table is a good option
- a puzzle board or velvet-like tablecloth to ensure the pieces won't slide around while you connect them
- PVA glue or varnish and a frame if you wish to keep the completed puzzle

Date Instructions

1. Choose a puzzle together for you to build. Any reasoning for the choice that calls to either of you is acceptable. It can be because you resonate with the imagery, because it contains your favorite things, or because the picture is attractive to you.

2. Set up your table with a puzzle board or velvet-like tablecloth.

3. Spend the date connecting all the puzzle pieces to create the whole picture. You may have your strategies for puzzles, but I find it helpful to start by completing the edges and then working inwards.

4. Once you have completed the puzzle, you have two options:

- Option 1: Take a photograph to remember your hard work, disconnect it, and pack it back into its box for future use.
- Option 2: Paint the top of the puzzle with PVA glue or varnish and allow it to dry. Don't apply it too thickly, or there will be discolored patches on the surface once it dries. Paint the bottom of the puzzle with more PVA glue for extra strength. Frame the finished and secured puzzle and display it on a wall where the two of you can admire it regularly and remember your achievement.

DATE NUMBER 40: NEW HOBBY TOGETHER

Sharing a hobby is a great way to build intimacy. Learning a new hobby allows you to learn something new together, allowing you and your partner to have a shared interest from now on, a sense of achievement, and a source of joy. There is no specific equipment listed for this date, as it will vary greatly depending on the hobby that you choose to discover.

Date Instructions

1. Spend some time discussing what hobbies you are interested in learning.

2. Choose one that interests both of you to move forward.

3. Organize any necessary equipment and book a date to start learning this hobby together. Also, consider booking an appointment with an instructor for more complex pursuits.

4. Consider reading up on it together or watching tutorials online before going on any practical elements.

5. Once you create or collect things for your new couple's hobby, keep it interesting by creating challenges for each other. Who can master a particular skill first or achieve the most in one session? You can support each other to learn parts that you or your partner find particularly challenging and share in the sense of accomplishment when you can both nail it. Hobbies that are great for couples include:

- learning to bake
- learning to brew beer or wine
- learning woodturning
- learning to canoe
- learning a musical instrument
- starting a collection of memorabilia for your favorite movie or TV show
- creating an array of sports memorabilia

DATE NUMBER 41: MATCH GAME

This game adds an element of unpredictability to your date in a safe environment with your partner. You can feel a sense of adventure right at home. It's also a great time to build intimacy by requesting favors that nurture your bond.

Suggested Equipment

- a deck of cards

Date Instructions

1. Deal four cards each to your partner and then yourself.

2. Place another four cards face up on the table between you.

3. Take turns matching the cards in your hand to those on the table.

4. Make pairs between those in your hand and those on the table; if you can successfully make a match, you can win that pair of cards and put them together to the side.

5. For each pair you win, you can ask your partner to do a favor for each pair you win. Have fun with your requests, and remember not to choose anything you

know will make your partner uncomfortable. Good examples can include:

- ask for a kiss
- ask them to make you a cup of coffee
- ask for a shoulder rub
- ask them to make up a poem for you
- if you are feeling spicy, you could request an article of their clothing

6. If you cannot match your cards to those on the table, you will have to drop one of your cards. Once your hand is empty, you can take another four cards from the deck. Likewise, replace the cards with another four once the table is open. The game ends once you deal last cards. The winner is the person who collects the most pairs during the game.

DATE NUMBER 42: NEW ADDRESS

This date is an opportunity for you to choose locations that you and your partner have memories of together or that you often frequent. The two of you will remember why these locations mean something special to you, and you will enjoy talking about your past experiences in each place together while building new memories.

Suggested Equipment

- pen and paper or a device to make a digital list

Date Instructions

1. Create a list of eight to ten sentimental locations you and your partner frequently visit. Choose places that will prompt fond memories, as well as familiar haunts. Suggestions for sites that you can use include the following:

- your favorite restaurant
- the spa or hair salon that either of you uses
- your favorite sports bar
- your partner's parent's home
- your best friend's address
- the place that you had your first date/kiss together
- the site that you got married
- your address

2. Write the addresses for each location, either on paper or digitally. At the end of your address list, include the address of the venue where your date will be that evening.

3. Give or send the list of addresses to your partner on the morning of your date night. Ask them to review the list throughout the day to see if they can remember or identify the places from the list.

4. That evening, visit a new location for a planned activity or dinner to create a recent memory together. You can spend some of the evening's conversation recalling the experiences or past dates you shared at your list addresses.

DATE NUMBER 43: BEDROOM PICNIC

This one can be as lavish or basic as your budget allows and can also be planned with very little notice if you need more time to organize one week. Despite the ease with which you can prepare for this activity, please don't underestimate how powerful it will be in cultivating your emotional bond with your partner. If you have plenty of time to organize, you can also pre-make some tasty treats with your partner a few days beforehand, taking note of the treats' shelf life.

Suggested Equipment

- blankets
- pillows
- a picnic basket

- some picnic utensils
- comfortable clothes
- a choice of soft romantic music
- a variety of picnic foods and treats
- some canned or bottled drinks

Date Instructions

1. Assemble your chosen foods and treats into your picnic basket. Don't forget to add your picnic utensils for an authentic picnic feel.

2. Spread a blanket over your bed or in a comfortable spot on the floor; make sure to lay out extra pillows for comfort if you choose the floor. Put on some romantic music playing softly as a background filler.

3. Allow your partner to get settled on the blanket while you go to retrieve your picnic basket.

4. Create a picnic spread as if at a park or a beach.

5. Make conversation while you eat; keep it light and entertaining. You could discuss the latest celebrity gossip or the upcoming release of favorite books or movies. Be sure to avoid topics like the house bills, work, or your responsibilities to your family, just for this evening.

6. Once you have finished your picnic, don't forget to proceed to dessert.

7. Aim to be as romantic as you can. You may want to consider the following ideas:

- Gifting a rose to your partner
- Take your picnic onto a balcony or yard to gaze at the stars.
- Offering your hand to dance

MOVING ON...

Congratulations! By now, you and your partner will have amassed some great activities to look back on and repeat, especially if you loved any of them. So here are the following category of date night ideas for you. The "crazy dates" are only for the brave, courageous, or those seeking to get cozier with their partners. The next chapter contains dates designed to encourage spontaneity, cultivate the courage to think outside the box and challenge you to invite more humor into your relationship.

7

THE CRAZY ACTIVITIES

An exciting date can stay in our memories forever. Sometimes it is the excitement that we remember about the date, but sometimes the intimacy and connection we felt in those moments make us feel the excitement again. Daring to do something random with your date nights can be very rewarding.

In 2019, Style Caster asked their readers to share stories of times when they felt their dates had hit the mark perfectly. The variety of stories they collected is a testament to how ideas are personalized. Here are three of my favorite anecdotes from their collection.

"Bar Hopping & Museum Kissing" This reader shared a first date that had culminated in a romantic kiss on the steps of the Brooklyn Museum. She recalled the close connection that the evening created with her partner. The couple visited three bars in one night, so it must have been a hectic evening, but she recalls it feeling like a dream.

"Do I Know You?": This reader recalls her and her partner's decision to spend an evening pretending they were on their first date. They held the doors open for one another, discussed all of the typical first date topics to get to know one another, and even opted to fit in the perfect first kiss. The reader recalls that the date felt very different and sweet.

"Italy Isn't So Far After All": This couple shared a dream of visiting Italy together to experience riding a Vespa and going on a gondola trip. For the reader, recalling the whole thing had been a total surprise and engrained in her memories—not only for the activity itself but for knowing that her partner had gone to the effort to research and plan the activities. Her partner even pretended it was a spur-of-the-moment decision to ask if she would like to visit Lake Merritt on their way home from dinner. But, when they arrived, he pointed out some gondolas to her. He had booked them a ride together, where the gondola driver sang Italian love songs to them. Her date had even brought along a bottle of champagne and truffles to share with her.

DATE NUMBER 44: THE $10 DATE

This date encourages you to step outside your comfort zone by handing the reins to your partner. It also lets you be competitive and have fun without breaking the bank.

Suggested Equipment

- Budget $10 each

Date Instructions

1. Visit a local thrift store together.

2. You must each shop for the other person using your $10 budget to create an outfit for the date.

3. To make things even more fun, consider making it more challenging by setting a theme for your outfits that you both have to follow. Ideas for themes can include

- a set color
- an era of fashion
- a holiday theme
- a trend or a style

4. Try on the clothes that you bought for one another. Try modeling them to see—maybe you can help each other to fasten ties, brooches, or do up zips, etc. Then take a few modeling-style photographs of each other to remember the day. Get creative and have fun trying out lots of different poses.

5. Once you have assembled your outfits and finished your photoshoot together, go to dinner in the same ensembles and take lots more photographs.

DATE NUMBER 45: CONJOINED BAKER

This challenges you to cooperate with your partner. It introduces a handicap to each of you that you must help each other overcome by working together on your baking project. It may be frustrating only to be allowed to use one of your arms, but it will also force you both to be creative in how you get around this problem and create an evening full of laughter.

Suggested Equipment

- a simple cake recipe
- ingredients as set out by your chosen recipe
- some additional decorative elements like writing, icing, or sprinkles

- essential baking equipment—mixing bowl, wooden spoon, measuring cups or jug, baking tin, cooling rack, and oven mitts
- a piece of ribbon

Date Instructions

1. You bake a cake together by sticking to each other's side and only using one hand each to perform the tasks necessary to complete your recipe. Don't also forget to decorate your cake—get creative and as bold as you can be in your choice of decorations.

2. You can consider holding hands to remind you not to use one hand each. If either of you forgets too often or don't think you can easily stick to this rule, tie your hands together using a ribbon. Be sure not to tie it too tightly and use a loose bow so that it is easy and quick to remove if necessary.

3. Cooperate to bake your cake; you may want to consider some of the following tips:

- one partner holds the bowl while the other adds ingredients or mixes
- both partners will lend a hand each to get the baking tray into and out of the oven
- one partner reaches for ingredients while the other measure them

DATE NUMBER 46: DANCING CHALLENGE

With the increased number of social media platforms, dance trends are sweeping worldwide via our mobile phones and computers. Dancing is not only a lot of fun, but it's excellent for your health, too. This date encourages you to spend quality time with your partner in a joint learning experience, which will build your trust in each other.

Suggested Equipment

- access to social media or YouTube for tutorials
- a device you can use to capture video footage

Date Instructions

1. Search online and choose a dance challenge or style to learn together. If you choose a style, you could also research some techniques that are common for that style.

2. Follow along with the videos you find, or take turns to learn a technique from your chosen style.

3. Once you feel like you have nailed the sequence, perform your dance together and record it to see how well you did.

4. If you feel brave, you can challenge each other to see who can perform the dance the best and upload your videos to social media.

DATE NUMBER 47: SHOW AND TELL

This date encourages you to think about the things that you appreciate about each other and share those precious feelings with your partner, too. It will help you express something to your partner that you might typically take for granted and let them know how you see them.

Suggested Equipment

- two shoe boxes or other boxes with lids

Date Instructions

1. Throughout the week before your date, collect some of your partner's items and store them in a shoe box or any other opaque box. Ask your partner to do the same with another box, and be sure not to peek at each other's collection before your date. Be sure that if you choose any items they use daily, you don't collect them until the day of your date, so they don't have to go without them when needed.

2. On your date night, you should bring your boxes.

3. Take turns taking an item out of your box. Show the object to your partner and explain to them how this item makes you feel about them, or share a memory about the object and how that memory with your partner makes you feel. For some inspiration, you could consider collecting some of the following items:

- books they read to your kids
- the aprons they use when making a special meal
- their hairbrush
- a sentimental piece of jewelry
- your wedding certificate or the children's birth certificates
- a souvenir from a holiday
- the clothes they wore on your first date

DATE NUMBER 48: GUESS WHAT

This date night will help your imagination run wild. You can choose the theme and the outcome as long as you are fully aware of your partner's likes and dislikes. There is no suggested equipment since this date depends on your choice. Decide together or separately what will be the theme of this date. You can make this funny, romantic, analytic, or all of the above.

Date Instructions

Choose one clothing article or an object you will bring to the date. Give the item to your partner earlier in the day. Ask your partner to come up with one or more ideas of how they "think" you will use this item during your date. You can also reverse roles, give them the option and let them choose what they "want" you to do using that item. The person offering the item is also responsible for coming up with their ideas. The partner receiving the article or object is responsible for handling the dinner for the date night. See how your thoughts come together or how you each think differently. Either way, choose one or two of the possible outcomes and enjoy. You can repeat this date and switch places next time.

The item you give to your partner could be anything. Here are a few examples:

- candle
- flower
- camera
- bath bombs
- essential oil
- eye/sleep mask
- hand bell
- wine

DATE NUMBER 49: DIFFICULT DATE

This date is a brilliant way to develop cooperation and teamwork with your partner. It will help the two of you tackle any lingering tasks that may have been causing you stress. It will foster trust and intimacy as you help get each other past a hurdle you have had trouble finishing on your own. The activities during this date depend highly on your chosen task; therefore, there isn't a specific list of suggested equipment.

Date Instructions

Speak with your partner about any tasks you have waiting for you to do that you may find daunting. Work as a team on the chore to improve the situation; you choose one you can complete together today.

Here are some examples of the tasks you may want to consider and some ideas for achieving them.

1. You do not have time to cook evening dinners or feel like you are relying on something other than eating out.

- Use your date night to meal prep together for the week ahead.
- Join together to create a meal plan and cook your chosen meals.

- Package and label the cooked meals in the fridge or freezer, ready for later reheating.
- Now, reward each other for a well-done job. Pour a glass of wine or grab some snacks, and relax together. Enjoy the rest of your evening with a sense of satisfaction.

2. The kids' rooms are messy, stressing you or your partner.

- With this one, it is the case that many hands make light work. Create a tag team together to clean and organize the room.
- Start by picking up all the clothes and putting them into the laundry or the cupboards if they are clean. One person can pick up all the items, and the other can sort them into the correct locations.
- Next, collect and dispose of any rubbish that has accumulated.
- Once the floor and surfaces are clear, consider moving any items that aren't used regularly into the garage.
- Lastly, freshen up the room together. One of you can clean and polish the surfaces, while the other person changes the bedding or vacuums.

- After you are happy with the state of the room, pop a simple dinner in the oven—something like a pizza is ideal. Treat yourselves to a cold drink and relax together for the rest of the evening.

3. The garage is jam-packed, and you don't have time to clear it.

- Work together to check and organize the items in the garage. Label boxes with one of three categories:

    - keep
    - donate/sell
    - toss

- Move each group of items to a different corner of the garage and decide who will take responsibility for the next steps.

    - Put away all of the items that you will be keeping.
    - Take the items to be thrown away outside to the trash.
    - Arrange to drop off donation items at a thrift store or charity center.

○ Take photographs and create listings for the items you want to sell. There are several online sales sites that you can use to advertise your items.

DATE NUMBER 50: CANDID CAMERA

This date takes a bit of preparation throughout the week, but the results will help you tell each other how much you appreciate each other. The date will foster an appreciation for each other and capture some memories you can keep forever.

Suggested Equipment

- a camera or mobile phone
- a larger screen device to display digital photos

Date Instructions

1. During the week before this date night, use a digital camera or mobile phone to snap photographs of your partner. Take pictures of everyday moments while they are doing things that remind you of why you fell in love with them. Ask your partner to do the same with you.

2. At the end of the week, download all your photographs to a shared device and prepare a computer monitor or television on which you can display them.

3. Sit down with some snacks and drinks; get comfortable with blankets and pillows if you want to cuddle while viewing the photographs.

4. Go through the photos, showing each other what you captured and telling your partner why you chose that moment to snap an image. Let each other know what you love about that moment and how it makes you feel about them. Some examples you could consider capturing, and the reasoning for them include:

- I love how you picked up and held our children while they were upset and calmed them down.
- I love how you took the initiative to take out the garbage without me asking you to do it first.
- I love the way you look while you are fixing dinner.
- I love watching you when you are still asleep in the morning.
- I love the smile on your face when you walk into the house after a long day.
- I love how your eyes light up while you practice your hobby.
- I love the care you put into preparing our children's baths.

DATE NUMBER 51: CRAZY FUN

This promotes laughter between you and your partner. When you are happy and laughing, the hormones you release will help make you feel connected. There is also the benefit that it can be an opportunity to blow off steam without regurgitating everything that went wrong this week but having fun together instead.

Suggested Equipment

- pen and paper or a digital device that you can store notes on
- a selection of DVDs—some comedy films and some TV series
- some clips of home videos where people are laughing and having fun

Date Instructions

1. Spend time lining up some jokes you can share with your partner on your date night. You can make up your own, take inspiration from TV shows or look for ideas online. Please note your chosen jokes on paper or in a digital format as long as they are easy to access. Ask your partner to collect a few tricks they would like to share.

2. Cook dinner together that evening, and tell your partner some of your jokes while you cook. Share the rest over your meal.

3. After dinner, sit on the couch to watch a comedy movie or some episodes of your favorite comedy series.

4. You can also re-watch old home videos or look online for videos of people laughing and having fun. Laughter is contagious, and it will encourage you both to let it out.

DATE NUMBER 52: THE BOXES

This date brings a sense of gratitude and appreciation for what you and your partner can do to help each other daily. Going through these tasks together helps you accomplish things that may be otherwise getting put off or forgotten about while showing support for your partner at the same time.

Suggested Equipment

- two boxes
- pen and paper

Date Instructions

1. After dinner on your date night, place two boxes on the table. Please discuss with your partner all the things you need to get done around the house, anything they can specifically do for you, and vice versa.

2. Cut some paper into seven small note-sized pieces and write each task down. Place your assignments in one of the boxes and your partner's duties in the other. Some of the chores you may want to consider including would be:

- sewing a button back onto a shirt
- calling to renew the car insurance
- taking the children to get their hair cut
- booking a doctor's appointment
- deep cleaning the freezer
- putting seasonal clothes that are going out of season right now in storage
- washing the cars

3. Once all the notes are in the boxes, swap your box with your partner.

4. In the week following your date night, take a note out of your box each day. Make it your mission to complete whatever task is written for your partner by the end of the day. You can celebrate a job well done

before bed with a glass of wine, an extra cuddle, or a kiss.

5. After each completed task, put the paper on your nightstand.

6. Revisit the boxes at the end of the week. Enjoy your success and spend that evening relaxing and indulging in each other's company, knowing that you have tackled some things you had been putting off.

MOVING ON...

Now you have all 52 interesting, exciting, and romantic date night ideas you and your partner can experience together. Many of them include cooking, snacks, or drinks. With that in mind, the following few chapters will give you some delicious recipes you can enjoy making with your partner.

PART III

LOVE RUNS THROUGH THE STOMACH

8

THE DATE NIGHT MEALS

Cooking is an intrinsic part of our everyday lives, and cooking fresh meals at home is known to have significant health benefits and help you keep your finances in check. On top of these incredible advantages, cooking with other people will help you strengthen your relationships. The meals you eat are often central to special occasions where people come together to celebrate. Because of this, the memories formed around the events are even more robust, as sight, smell, hearing, and taste all create their little record of the event in your memories. You associate the enjoyment of that time with the foods and reminisce about them whenever you smell or taste them again.

Below are some examples of how creating positive associations with such memories and cooking can boost your relationship with your partner:

1. When you enjoy cooking with your partner, it deepens the bond between you while you practice cooperation and patience with one another. You can learn to enjoy creating meals for each other and your family, especially when you appreciate each other's company.
2. Cooking with your partner creates many opportunities to create precious memories together. Similar to having a favorite dish that may remind you of childhood because it tastes "just like mama used to make," you can create more new favorites that remind you of your partner and the quality time you enjoyed together in the kitchen.
3. Cooking forces you to slow down and concentrate on the task in front of you; if you don't, the chances are you will end up with a burnt dinner. It will give you some time to create mental clarity as you focus on dinner for 30 minutes to an hour; you won't need to balance your other tasks.
4. Whether new to you or a practiced favorite, your cooking together can be a force for

learning. It will help you brush up on your math skills, cultural awareness as you try cuisines from around the world, and creativity when you plan your meals together.
5. When you and your partner cook together, you must communicate to get the job done well. Regularly cooking with your partner will foster your ability to work together as a team and develop your communication skills to work more effectively. Once you are in sync with one another in the kitchen, you will notice your verbal communication becoming less frequent as you focus more on each other's body language for direction.

ONE DISH ROAST PORK

Servings: 4

Ingredients Needed

- 1 lb pork loin joint with some top fat
- 1 cup carrots
- 7 oz or 4–5 large Yukon Gold potatoes
- 4 tablespoon olive oil
- 1 tablespoon un-set honey of choice
- 1 teaspoon basil
- 1 teaspoon oregano

- 1 teaspoon kosher salt
- 1 teaspoon ground black pepper
- 3 cloves garlic, minced
- 1–2 cups sweet cider
- 2 apples of choice
- 1 tablespoon cornstarch
- extra salt and black pepper for seasoning

Instructions

1. Preheat your oven to 350°F.
2. Make a rub for the meat by mixing one teaspoon of oil with three cloves of minced garlic, one teaspoon of basil, oregano, kosher salt, and ground black pepper. Set this aside.
3. Peel and rough chop the potatoes into 1–1.5 inch chunks. Par-boil in a saucepan with a pinch of salt to season them for 5–10 minutes or until a knife will easily pierce them, but they don't fall apart when tested.
4. While the potatoes boil, prepare your meat by scoring the top fat diagonally with a knife and crossing the scores to make a diamond pattern. Place the meat on a chopping board or cooking rack over the sink and pour hot water over the fat to encourage the top layer to contract and open the scores you have made. For safety, do

not be tempted to hold the meat in your hand while you do this.
5. Pat the meat dry with a kitchen towel and place it in a large roasting dish. Pour the previously prepared rub over the top. Rub it into all the scores and down the sides of the joint.
6. Pour sweet cider into the base of the oven dish. The liquid should rise no more than 1 inch up the side of your joint. Place a lid on the dish—or wrap it with tin foil—and put it in the oven for 15 minutes.
7. Meanwhile, drain your potatoes but leave them in your saucepan. Hold the lid on the pan and shake it to break up the outside edges of your potatoes for a nice crispy roast. Pour in 2 tablespoons of olive oil and gently stir to coat the potatoes, then set them to the side.
8. Slice your carrots in half lengthways and parboil them in the same pot as before. When you drain them, a small amount of the potato will be left in the pan that will coat them and help them roast. The parboil aims to soften the carrot a little before roasting, not to cook them through. Repeat the drain and shake process you did with the potatoes for the carrots. Do not add oil to the carrots—instead, stir in the honey.

9. Cut your apples into six pieces and remove the seeds. Rub a small amount of olive oil on all of the cut surfaces.
10. Remove the pork from the oven and remove the lid. Place the carrots, potatoes, and apples around the pork in the pot's base. It is okay if they touch, but try not to pile them up on top of each other. At this stage, there will still be cider left in the bottom of the dish, so take care not to splash it as it will be boiling.
11. Return the oven dish to the oven without a lid for 45–50 minutes. You are aiming for the crackling to be golden brown and the joint to have an internal temperature of 145°F.
12. Remove the meat from the dish and set it aside to rest.
13. Remove the vegetables and apples and also set them aside.
14. Boil 1 cup of water and pour it into the oven dish. Use a spatula or wooden spoon to lift all the fond—the browned and caramelized drippings from your meat. Stir until it is well mixed. Transfer the contents into the same saucepan used for the potatoes and carrots and heat on low heat for 2 minutes to pick up any honey residue.

15. In a cup or ramekin, mix one tablespoon of water with one tablespoon of cornstarch to form a thin paste. Pour this into the saucepan, mix in thoroughly and cook it out for 3–5 minutes. The sauce will thicken and become more gravy-like in texture.
16. Pour the gravy into a serving jug.
17. Carve the pork into slices and place it onto a large plate or platter. Arrange the carrots, potatoes, and apples around the meat and serve in the center of a table with the gravy, allowing everyone to plate their meals.

SHRIMP RISOTTO

Servings: 2

Ingredients Needed

- 2 tablespoons olive oil
- 1 sweet onion
- 2 tablespoons unsalted butter
- 4 oz mushrooms
- 1 clove garlic
- 1 teaspoon thyme
- ¾ cup risotto or Arborio rice
- 1 tablespoon lemon zest

- juice of ½ a lemon or 1 teaspoon of concentrated lemon juice
- 1 cup white wine
- 3 cup chicken broth
- ¾ lb shrimp, peeled and deveined
- 1 cup grated parmesan cheese
- salt and ground black pepper

Instructions

1. Use 1 tablespoon of olive oil in a pot to brown the shrimp on medium-high heat for 1 minute. The aim isn't to cook the shrimp through at this point, only to brown them. Once browned on both sides, set aside for later.
2. Dice your onion and slice the mushrooms. Mince the garlic roughly with a knife.
3. Use the same pot and another tablespoon of olive oil, and heat on medium-high heat until it sizzles. Then add the onions and garlic; cook until the onions become transparent.
4. Add the butter, thyme, and mushrooms to the pan and cook down the mushrooms. They will reduce by approximately half the size.
5. Add the risotto rice to the pan and stir gently to toast it.

6. Add the lemon zest and juice, then turn the heat to medium. Continue stirring and add the white wine. Cook for 5–7 minutes or until most of the wine has cooked off. Now is when patience comes into play, so don't be tempted to turn the heat back up to cook off the wine.
7. Slowly add ½ cup of chicken broth. Continue stirring until the rice has absorbed all of the broth. Don't add extra stock until the rice has completely absorbed the previous cup.
8. Add another ½ cup of chicken broth and continue stirring. Repeat adding ½ cup of broth whenever the rice absorbed the previous cups. Keep an eye on the consistency of your risotto; it should be creamy and have a sheen to it; you may need to add extra broth if it becomes dull and cooks out too fast. Keep repeating until the rice cooks entirely and no liquid remains.
9. Season generously with salt and pepper.
10. Add the shrimp to the pan and cook for 2–3 minutes. Remove the pan from the heat and stir the parmesan cheese to combine.
11. Serve immediately with extra parmesan sprinkled on top to taste.

CHICKEN PARMESAN

Servings: 2

Ingredients Needed

- 2 large skinless chicken breasts
- 2 eggs, beaten
- ⅔ cup breadcrumbs
- ⅔ cup parmesan cheese, grated
- 1 tablespoon olive oil
- 2 garlic cloves, crushed
- 1 ½ cup passata
- 1 teaspoon baker's sugar
- 1 teaspoon dried oregano
- ½ cup light mozzarella, torn

Instructions

1. Tenderize the chicken breast by placing it in a zip-top plastic bag, then pound it with a rolling pin or the flat side of a meat mallet until the breast is ½ inch thick.
2. Dip the flattened chicken breast into your two beaten eggs, then coat them with your breadcrumbs and half of the parmesan.
3. In a small pan, heat 1 tablespoon olive oil and 2 cloves of crushed garlic for 1 minute. Add 1 ½

cups of passata, 1 teaspoon of baker's sugar, and 1 teaspoon of dried oregano. Season this mixture with salt and pepper to taste and allow it to simmer for 5 to 10 minutes.
4. Using olive oil, heat your skillet on medium heat before placing your breaded chicken breasts into the pan for 2–3 minutes on each side until golden brown.
5. Place your browned chicken breasts onto a baking pan or dish, topping them with mozzarella and a layer of passata sauce. Bake for 13–15 minutes, then sprinkle your remaining parmesan on top before broiling on high for an additional minute until the cheese is bubbling and brown.
6. Serve and enjoy.

SLOW COOKED BEEF STEW

Servings: 6

Ingredients Needed

- 2 lb stewing steak
- 2 tablespoons olive oil
- 1 cup red wine
- 5 cups beef stock
- 5 oz carrots, sliced

- 5 oz turnip, chopped into ¼-inch cubes
- 5 oz Yukon Gold potato, chopped into ¼-inch cubes
- 5 oz broccoli, rough chopped
- 1 lb button mushroom, cut in ¼
- 1 large onion, chopped
- 1 teaspoon ground black pepper
- 1 teaspoon salt
- 1 teaspoon oregano
- 1 teaspoon basil
- 2 cloves garlic, minced
- 1 tablespoon cornstarch

Instructions

1. Warm the olive oil in the base of a pot on medium-high heat until it becomes clear.
2. Brown the steak on all sides in the pot, remove it and set it aside for later.
3. Add the onions, herbs, and garlic into the pot and cook the onions until they become translucent.
4. Add the steak to the pot and sprinkle with cornstarch; stir to coat all pieces.
5. Add 1 cup of beef stock and stir to combine all the flavors.

6. Add the remaining vegetables to the pot, then pour the wine and the rest of the beef stock over the top. If the stock and wine don't cover all of the solids in your stew, you can add some extra water to be sure that everything is submerged.
7. Bring the liquid to a boil, then reduce heat to medium-low.
8. Cover with a lid and let the stew simmer for at least 3 hours. Check and stir once every 30 minutes to prevent sticking at the bottom. The liquid should always cover the solid ingredients; if the level drops too low, add more water, ½ cup at a time.
9. Serve with a starchy side of your choice (i.e., dinner rolls, mashed potatoes, rice, etc.).

RAINBOW VEGETABLE CURRY

Servings: 4

Ingredients Needed

- 1 large onion
- 2 cloves garlic
- 2 tablespoon vegetable oil
- 1 zucchini
- ½ butternut squash or 1 large sweet potato

- ½ red pepper
- 1 small cauliflower
- 2 tablespoon tomato paste
- 1 can of chopped tomatoes
- 1 ½ cups of vegetable stock
- 1 can chickpeas
- 2 handfuls of spinach
- 1 teaspoon ground coriander
- 1 teaspoon ground cumin
- ½ teaspoon turmeric
- ½ teaspoon chili powder
- 1 teaspoon paprika
- 1 teaspoon garam masala
- 1 star anise
- 1 stick cinnamon

Instructions

1. Finely chop your onions and garlic and add them into a pot with oil to gently saute them for roughly 8 minutes.
2. Separate your cauliflower florets, chop the zucchini, peel and dice the squash or sweet potato, and chop your red pepper.
3. Add your now-prepared vegetables to your sauteed onions and garlic, covering them with a lid for roughly 5 minutes while you measure

and mix your spices.
4. Add your spice mixture to the vegetables.
5. Stir for 1 minute before adding your tomato paste, stir for another minute, and then add your chopped tomatoes and just enough vegetable stock to cover your vegetables.
6. Season with salt before bringing to a boil, and allow to simmer for 30–45 minutes until the vegetables have become tender.
7. Drain your chickpeas before adding them to the curry. Turn the heat down and cook until the sauce reaches your preferred thickness.
8. Add your spinach and mix throughout before adding the lid and cooking for a minute. Then turn off the heat.
9. Allow your curry to rest while covered for a few minutes for the spinach to wilt.
10. Serve with basmati rice.

SALMON EN PAPILLOTE

Servings: 2

Ingredients Needed

- 2 4oz salmon filets
- 1 lemon, juice only
- 1 lemon, thinly sliced

- ¼ cup green onions, chopped
- 4 spears of fresh asparagus, cut into 1 ½ inch pieces
- 4 teaspoons of olive oil

Instructions

1. Preheat your oven to 350°F.
2. Squeeze a lemon over your salmon filets, then lightly sprinkle with salt and pepper.
3. Fold two pieces of parchment paper in half crosswise, placing a salmon filet on one side of each piece of paper.
4. Place 1 to 2 lemon slices on each piece of fish, and surround each with two of your cut asparagus spears.
5. Sprinkle your chopped green onions over the lemon slices, and fold the parchment paper over your salmon filets.
6. Carefully fold the open edges of your parchment paper over multiple times to seal your salmon inside an envelope. Do not use tape to secure the paper closed.
7. Place your salmon parcels onto a baking sheet before lightly brushing the tops of each envelope with olive oil.

8. Bake in your preheated oven for 20 to 25 minutes, until the asparagus is tender and the salmon has become opaque and slightly flaky.
9. To serve, place the parcel onto your plate and cut it open, releasing the aroma.

CREAMY BAKED MACARONI AND CHEESE

Servings: 4

Ingredients Needed

- 1lb of any short dry pasta
- ½ cup salted butter
- ½ cup of all-purpose flour
- 1 cup of heavy cream
- 2 cups of milk
- 2 cups of shredded white cheddar
- 2 cups of shredded sharp cheddar
- 2 cups of shredded gruyere (optionally, you can replace it with 2 cups of shredded cheddar)
- ½ teaspoon paprika
- ½ teaspoon garlic powder
- ½ teaspoon onion powder
- salt and pepper to taste
- ½ cup breadcrumbs
- ½ cup shredded parmesan cheese

Instructions

1. To prepare, start by shredding your cheese and setting it aside.
2. Bring a large pot of water to a boil. Once the water is boiling, add salt and pour in the pasta. Cook until al dente.
3. In another large pot, melt your butter. Once the butter is completely melted but not browned, add in the flour and cook for 1 minute, constantly stirring.
4. Slowly pour the heavy cream and milk, whisking the mixture to avoid clumping.
5. Mix in your paprika, garlic powder, onion powder, and salt and pepper to taste.
6. Turn off the heat and fold in your shredded cheese. Continue stirring until you reach a smooth, thick consistency. (If you need to loosen up the sauce, slowly spoon in some of the starchy pasta water in small amounts, taking care not to make it too liquidy)
7. Add your cooked pasta to the cheese sauce and mix well, coating all the pasta in your luxurious sauce.
8. Butter a baking dish and pour in your pasta and cheese mixture. Top this with breadcrumbs and shredded parmesan cheese.

9. Bake in the oven at 350 for 15 minutes or until the top is golden brown and the cheese is bubbling.
10. Remove from the oven and let sit for 10 minutes, then serve with an optional side salad

MUSHROOM STROGANOFF

Servings: 2

Ingredients Needed

- 1 oz butter
- 1 tablespoon olive oil
- 1 large sliced onion
- 1 lb sliced mushrooms
- ½ teaspoon garlic puree
- 1 teaspoon ground paprika
- 1 pinch of chili powder
- 2 fl oz white wine
- 1 oz tomato puree
- 3 ½ fluid oz vegetable stock
- 3 ½ fluid oz cream
- ½ teaspoon chopped parsley

Instructions

1. Melt your butter and oil in a large pot.
2. Add in your vegetables, garlic puree, spices, and wine before cooking until the mushrooms are tender and golden brown and your onions are soft.
3. Stir in your tomato puree, vegetable stock, and cream.
4. Bring to a boil, then reduce heat to a simmer, adding the parsley.
5. Simmer until your stroganoff reaches your desired thickness.
6. Serve with rice.

BEEF RAGU

Servings: 4

Ingredients Needed

- 4 tablespoons olive oil
- 2 lbs chuck steak, cut into ¾-inch pieces
- 1 brown onion, finely chopped
- 1 garlic clove, crushed
- 4 sticks of celery, finely chopped
- 1 tablespoon chopped fresh rosemary
- 1 ½ cups red wine

- 3 cups tomato passata
- 1 ¾ oz dry pappardelle pasta per person

Instructions

1. Preheat the oven to 320°F.
2. Heat olive oil in a large, oven-safe pan over medium heat.
3. Season your meat, adding it to your heated pan and browning it on all sides.
4. Remove the beef and set it to the side.
5. Add your garlic, celery, onion, and rosemary to your pan, cooking them until they are soft.
6. Return your meat to the pan, add the red wine, and boil it.
7. Stir in the passata and cover the surface of your ragu with a circle of parchment paper.
8. Bake for 2 ½ hours or until the meat is very tender.
9. Remove the parchment paper, breaking up the meat with a fork.
10. Season with salt and pepper to taste before setting aside.
11. Cook your pappardelle in salted boiling water until it is al dente.

12. In a saute pan, combine 3 tablespoons of your ragu per portion of pasta and a tablespoon of your pasta water.
13. Cook on low heat, tossing it together until the sauce clings to the pasta.
14. Serve with grated parmesan and freshly ground pepper.

TURKEY BURGERS

Servings: 4

Ingredients Needed

- 1 lb ground turkey
- 1 small onion, diced
- 1 clove of garlic, minced
- 1 egg
- 1 tablespoon olive oil
- iceberg or romaine lettuce to serve
- large beef tomato slices to serve
- 4 burger buns

Instructions

1. Combine the ground meat, diced onion, garlic, and egg in a large mixing bowl.

2. Generously season the meat mixture with salt and pepper.
3. Rub some olive oil on your hands to prevent sticking, then split the mixture into 4 and shape each ¼ into a ball between your palms.
4. Warm some oil in a skillet on medium heat. Once it bubbles gently, place the meatballs onto the skillet and press down to form burger patties.
5. Cook medium heat for 4–6 minutes on each side. Be sure not to turn the heat up to cook faster as turkey can be prone to drying, so slow and steady is better. The internal temperature should be 165°F.
6. Toast your burger buns and top them with your favorite condiments, some lettuce, and a slice of tomato.
7. Add the turkey burgers to the bun and enjoy a side of fries, chips, or a salad.

MOVING ON…

Cooking meals together with your partner can be life-changing for your relationship. The benefits can often speak volumes for themselves by capitalizing on an opportunity to spend quality time together daily while you prepare dinner to learn to share a new hobby.

However, adding some extra pizzazz through desserts and drinks is still possible to up the ante on your everyday meals and date nights. In the next chapter, you will find some delicious treat recipes to work on together and deliver something extra to the table.

9

THE DATE NIGHT DESSERTS AND DRINKS

Regarding cooking with your partner, you may be surprised that 70% of married couples who participated in a relationship survey stated they enjoy cooking together. The same study also reported that those couples who do this conveyed higher satisfaction levels in other areas of their lives than those who don't share the kitchen (Martell, 2014). Couples who cook together are better communicators and share a more profound sense of intimacy and trust than those who don't. Suppose the magic hasn't yet convinced you to produce dinners together. In that case, the desserts and drinks in this chapter will help you glean the benefits of this shared time cooperating in the same instant as bringing some extra sweetness to your date nights.

CHEESECAKE FOR TWO

Servings: 2

Specific Equipment Needed

- muffin tin
- paper cake liners

Ingredients Needed

- 2 graham crackers
- 1 tablespoon melted butter
- 3 tablespoons sour cream
- 6 tablespoons cream cheese
- 3 tablespoons sugar, plus 1 teaspoon sugar for the base
- 1 large egg
- 2 teaspoons all-purpose flour
- ½ teaspoon lemon zest
- a squeeze of lemon juice
- ½ teaspoon vanilla extract
- pinch of salt
- 1 teaspoon strawberry jam
- 2 large strawberries

Instructions

1. Preheat the oven to 325°F.
2. Line two cups in a muffin tray with paper liners.
3. Use a food processor set on the pulse to combine the graham crackers, butter, and one teaspoon of sugar. If you don't have a food processor, you can crush the crackers in a freezer or sandwich bag with a rolling pin and then mix them by hand.
4. Divide the cracker crumb mixture in two and press it down into the base of the paper liners.
5. Bake the crumb bases for 8 minutes or until they become lightly golden in color.
6. Remove the muffin tray from the oven and allow the bases to cool completely before adding the fillings.
7. Mix the cream cheese, sour cream, salt, vanilla extract, lemon zest, sugar, and egg in a mixing bowl or food processor until the mixture is light and creamy.
8. Divide the cheese mixture between the two liners.
9. Fill the remaining empty sections of the muffin tray with water, then bake for 25–30 minutes, or until the center is set but still able to jiggle.

10. Cool the cheesecakes inside the tin until they are at room temperature. Then pop the liners out of the tray and refrigerate overnight.
11. When ready to serve, finely dice two strawberries and stir them into a teaspoon of strawberry jam with a squeeze of lemon juice. Plate the cheesecake and top it with the strawberry topping.

INDIVIDUAL STRAWBERRY TRIFLES

Servings: 2

Ingredients Needed

- 10 vanilla wafers
- 2 cups strawberries, cut into ¼
- juice of one lemon
- 1 tablespoon granulated sugar
- 3 cups heavy cream
- 1 teaspoon vanilla extract
- ¼ cup confectioner's sugar
- ⅓ cup amaretto liqueur
- 1 teaspoon demerara sugar

Instructions

1. Place the strawberries in a mixing bowl and add the lemon juice. Stir together and leave to sit for 15 minutes.
2. Add the granulated sugar to the strawberries and mix to coat all the cut surfaces. Leave to marinade for another 5 minutes.
3. Add the cream, confectioner's sugar, and vanilla extract to a separate bowl. Whip it with a whisker or an electric mixer until it forms a soft peak.
4. Using two highball glasses, assemble the trifles—layer vanilla wafers in the bottom of the glasses. Use 3–4 wafers in each glass, depending on its size.
5. Brush amaretto liqueur over the vanilla wafers, and top it with 1–2 tablespoons of marinated strawberries.
6. Using a separate spoon, add a dollop of whipped cream on top of the strawberries in each glass.
7. Repeat the layering process. Divide the remaining ingredients between the two glasses: vanilla wafers, strawberries, and cream.
8. Once the glasses are loaded, use the demerara sugar to garnish the last cream layer.

9. Place the trifles in the fridge until you are ready to serve. They are best when chilled for at least one hour.

CHOCOLATE MOUSSE

Servings: 6

Specific Equipment Needed

- 6 6 oz ramekins or dessert glasses

Ingredients Needed

- 7 oz Dark chocolate
- 2 ½ cups heavy cream
- ¼ cup granulated sugar, plus an extra 2 tablespoons for the cream mix
- ¼ teaspoon salt
- 3 egg yolks
- ½ teaspoon espresso powder
- 1 ½ teaspoon vanilla extract
- extra chocolate shavings and raspberries to serve

Instructions

1. Chop the chocolate finely to improve melt time.

2. In a mixing bowl, add the egg yolks and ¼ cup sugar. Whisk until all the sugar blends into the eggs.
3. Add one cup of heavy cream with the salt to a small saucepan and boil on medium heat. Once the cream starts to simmer, remove it from the heat.
4. Take ¼ cup of the warm cream and slowly drizzle it into the egg mixture. Continuously whisk while doing so to prevent the eggs from splitting.
5. Once thoroughly combined, pour the egg mixture into the saucepan with the rest of the cream. Continue whisking to combine all the ingredients.
6. Return the saucepan to medium-low heat and continue mixing until it thickens enough to coat the sides of the pan.
7. Remove the mixture from the heat and add chocolate and espresso powder. Stir quickly until all the chocolate melts.
8. Transfer the chocolate mixture to a bowl and place in the fridge for 20 minutes. Stir it halfway through.
9. Mix 1 ½ cups of cream, 2 tablespoons of sugar, and vanilla extract in a large mixing bowl. Whisk the mixture until it forms soft peaks.

10. Add a large spoonful of the cream mixture to the chocolate mixture and stir to combine. Once fully incorporated, pour the remaining cream into the chocolate mixture and gently fold it together.
11. Divide the mixture between six 6 oz ramekins or into dessert glasses. Refrigerate for one hour.
12. To serve, whip the remaining cream and make some chocolate shavings. Top the chocolate mouse with whipped cream, chocolate, and fresh raspberries.

RED VELVET MUG CAKE

Servings: 2

Specific Equipment Needed

- 2 microwave-safe mugs

Ingredients Needed

- 2 tablespoons cocoa powder
- ½ teaspoon baking powder
- ½ teaspoon salt
- ½ cup all-purpose flour
- 6 tablespoons granulated sugar
- 4 tablespoon vegetable oil

- 1 teaspoon apple cider vinegar
- 6 tablespoons milk
- ½ teaspoon vanilla extract, plus an extra dash for the topping
- 24 drops of red food coloring
- 4 tablespoons cream cheese
- 2 tablespoons confectioner's sugar

Instructions

1. Mix the ingredients for the cake directly inside two microwave-safe mugs. Split each wet element between the mugs, starting with the milk, vinegar, and food coloring. Stir until completely incorporated.
2. Add the vegetable oil and vanilla extract to each mug and stir to combine.
3. Now split the dry ingredients between the mugs. Start by adding the flour and thoroughly mix it into the wet mixture until there are no lumps.
4. Split the granulated sugar, cocoa powder, baking powder, and salt between the mugs and stir again to combine.
5. Microwave the mugs individually for 1 ½ minute. When the cake is ready, a toothpick

inserted into the center will come out free of batter or crumbs.
6. Allow cooling for 2–3 minutes while you make the topping.
7. Mix the cream cheese, vanilla extract, and confectioner's sugar in a mixing bowl.
8. Beat the cream mixture until it is smooth, then split it in half and spoon it over the mug cakes.

MOLTEN CHOCOLATE CAKE FOR TWO

Servings: 2

Specific Equipment Needed

- 2 6-oz ramekins
- heavy-bottom saucepan

Ingredients Needed

- ¼ cup all-purpose flour
- ½ cup confectioner's sugar
- 4 tablespoons butter
- 2 oz dark chocolate
- 1 egg plus one egg yolk

Instructions

1. Preheat the oven to 450°F.
2. Prepare for other recipe steps by lightly buttering the ramekins on the bottoms and sides, then finely chop the chocolate to improve later.
3. In a saucepan, melt the butter. Once melted, remove from the heat.
4. Stir the chopped chocolate into the butter until it has also melted. Set aside while you move on to preparing the eggs.
5. In a mixing bowl, place one egg and one egg yolk. Whisk them together until they form a uniform color.
6. Add the confectioner's sugar to the eggs and whisk until combined and smooth.
7. Add the chocolate mixture into the mixing bowl and whisk to combine.
8. Add the flour to your mixing bowl and stir it in until the mixture is smooth and free from any lumps.
9. Pour it into your prepared ramekins and bake in the oven for 10–13 minutes. The tops will crack open when it is ready.
10. Use a knife to free the chocolate cakes from the sides of the ramekins, then flip them onto a

plate to serve. You can add vanilla ice cream and fresh raspberries for an extra treat.

THE MAGIC OF COCKTAILS

Mixed drinks and cocktails can add flare to a meal. They are often simpler to make than you might expect—and once you understand the basics, your partner can experiment with you to create a new signature drink that matches each of your tastes. A few golden rules when making cocktails are

1. Don't skip the ice; recipes include ice in different forms for a reason. Ice doesn't just cool drinks. The type and amount used will control the level of dilution a drink gets in perfect balance with its other ingredients.
2. Always follow the recommended preparation. Shaken, stirred, muddled, or blended, much like using the correct amount of ice, it controls how much a drink's components are mixed. Skipping out on the recommended preparation type can alter the taste.
3. Garnish is your friend; some people will tell you that skipping garnish is fine, and though it isn't a disastrous outcome if you don't have the ingredients handy, it can affect the overall taste

of a drink. Choosing the correct garnish can cut through the sweetness of a drink or take the edge off a sharp-tasting recipe.

Frozen Martini

Servings: 4

Specific Equipment Needed

- blender
- 4 cocktail sticks

Ingredients Needed

- 1 cup dry gin
- 1 cup ice
- 2 oz blanc vermouth
- 2 oz dry vermouth
- ¼ tablespoon orange bitters
- 8 green olives, pitted

Instructions

1. Add the ice and all measurements of the wet ingredients into the blender. Mix using the pulse setting on the machine until the mixture becomes white and slushy.

2. Split the mixture between 4 glasses. Pierce two olives onto each cocktail stick and add one stick to each glass for garnish. Serve immediately.

Mixed Berry Cosmopolitan

Servings: 1

Specific Equipment Needed

- cocktail shaker
- cocktail stick

Ingredients Needed

- 1 ½ oz strawberry vodka
- ½ oz Chambord
- 3 oz pomegranate juice
- a squeeze of lime juice
- One strawberry
- 1 cup ice

Instructions

- Remove the stalks and cut the strawberry in half. Skewer the pieces onto a cocktail stick sideways, so they resemble tiny hearts.

- Add ice, vodka, Chambord, and lime juice into a cocktail shaker. Shake it up for 30–60 seconds.
- Pour the liquid into a glass, straining out the ice.
- Add a squeeze of lime juice on top and garnish by balancing the strawberry stick across the rim of the glass.

Gimlet

Servings: 2

Specific Equipment Needed

- cocktail shaker

Ingredients Needed

- 2 tablespoon sugar, plus extra for garnish
- 2 tablespoon water
- juice of 2 limes, plus two slices for garnish
- 6 oz dry gin
- 2 cup ice

Instructions

1. Begin by making your simple syrup—heat equal measures of granulated sugar and water in a

saucepan. For this recipe, you will need 2 tablespoons of each; however, you can make larger quantities and store them in the fridge for up to 10 days. Heat the mixture until the sugar dissolves, but the liquid remains clear.
2. Next, prepare two glasses for serving. Sprinkle some sugar onto a small plate and pour a small amount of simple syrup onto a second small plate. Dip the rim of the glasses into the syrup, and then place the rim of the glass into the sugar, turning it gently to coat the edge evenly with the sugar.
3. Add 1 cup of ice, 1 tablespoon of simple syrup, the juice of one lime, and 3 oz dry gin into a cocktail shaker. Shake well to combine for up to 60 seconds.
4. Strain the liquid into one glass, disposing of the remaining ice. Then repeat the mixing step to fill the second glass.
5. Garnish both glasses with a slice of lime each.

Fruity Sangria

Servings: 4

Specific Equipment Needed

- pitcher

- 4 highball glasses

Ingredients Needed

- 1 bottle of your favorite red wine—if you are unsure, cabernet sauvignon is a good base for this drink
- ⅓ cup pomegranate juice
- ⅓ cup of your favorite bourbon—Use Southern Comfort if you prefer the sangria to be sweeter
- 1 tablespoon honey
- 1 crisp apple
- 1 peach
- ½ lb cherries
- 2 cups ice

Instructions

1. Prepare the fruit by pitting and cutting the cherry in half, slicing the apple into thin rounds, removing the core, and chopping the rounds in half; then, pit and dice the peach into ¼ pieces.
2. Pour the bottle of red wine into the pitcher, then add the pomegranate juice and bourbon. Give it a quick stir to combine.

3. Add the honey to the pitcher and stir until it dissolves.
4. Add all of the prepared fruit into the pitcher and give it another quick stir.
5. Chill the whole mixture for at least one hour.
6. To serve, divide the ice between 4 highball glasses. Then pour the sangria over the top, allowing some fruit into each glass.

Russian Bellini

Servings: 2

Specific Equipment Needed

- 2 champagne flutes

Ingredients Needed

- 12 oz prosecco
- 2 oz rye vodka
- 2 oz peach puree
- peach slices to garnish

Instructions

1. Place 1 oz vodka and 1 oz peach puree into the bottom of each champagne flute. Gently muddle them together with a spoon.
2. Carefully top each glass with 6 oz of prosecco; this will result in a gentle color gradient from the peach puree at the bottom to clear prosecco at the top.
3. Garnish each glass with a slice of peach on the rim, then serve.

MOVING ON...

Now you have a base of fun and easy-to-learn dessert and drink recipes that can help you and your partner brew up a storm on your date nights. Lastly, I will recap the tools you now have at your disposal to rekindle the magic of your relationship.

CONCLUSION

You have gone through the science and magic of a healthy relationship, reminded yourself why your partnership is unique and worth fighting for and given a year's worth of date night ideas to kick-start your journey into a more exciting, engaging, and rewarding time together. It's time to get out there and break any mundane routines you may have settled for, learn better communication with your partner through fun activities, and give and gain higher satisfaction from quality interactions.

The shared recipes are a great starting point to keep your date nights going and remove some anxiety from choosing what to cook or learning to cook before the rest of the date can even begin. You now have bountiful ideas for activities, and delicious food can help you create new memories.

You can build a lasting connection with your partner and have fun doing it, too! Successful dates are within reach and don't need to be intimidating. Spontaneous examples of how much you care for each other can be just as fulfilling as carefully pre-planned date nights. Whatever you decide to do, as long as you keep a regular commitment to spending time together, you can glean the benefits of a stronger emotional connection.

So, don't wait. Please remember that only some things have to go as planned for you and your partner to make great memories together. Use your newfound knowledge to embrace the ups and downs of daily life with your partner as a team.

The sooner you set a date together and break the ice to make date nights a routine, the sooner you and your partner can enjoy the beautiful rewards of creating a healthy space for your relationship together. Go out there and conquer the battlefield of love the right way, make new memories, and challenge each other to create a buzz of excitement around any time you have planned together.

Please consider leaving a review for the book where you purchased it, and share how you get along with any of the dates you try from this book.

SUPPORTING INFORMATION LISTS

AMERICA'S FAVORITE SITCOMS: INSPIRATION LIST

The Big Bang Theory, 2007–2019. Created by Chuck Lorre and Bill Prady for CBS. Starring Johnny Galecki and Jim Parsons.

Black-ish, 2014–Ongoing. Created by Kenya Barris for ABC. Starring Anthony Anderson and Tracee Ellis Ross.

The Carmichael Show, 2015–2017. Created by David Caspe for NBC. Starring Jerrod Carmichael and Amber Stevens.

Cheers, 1982–1992. Created by Glen and Les Charles and James Burrows for NBC. Starring Ted Danson and Shelly Long.

Frasier, 1992–2004. Created by David Angell, Peter Casey, and David Lee for NBC. Starring Kelsey Grammer and Jane Leeves.

Fresh Prince of Bel-Air, 1990–1996. Created by Andy and Susan Borowitz for NBC. Starring Will Smith and James Avery.

Friends, 1994–2004. Created by David Crane and Marta Kauffman for NBC. Starring Jennifer Aniston and Courtney Cox.

Good Times, 1974–1979. Created by Eric Monte, Mike Evans, and Norman Lear for CBS. Starring Esther Rolle and John Amos.

How I Met Your Mother, 2005–2014. Created by Carter Bays and Craig Thomas for ABC. Starring Josh Randor and Jason Segel.

Malcolm in the Middle, 2000–2005. Created by Linwood Boomer for Fox. Starring Jane Kaczmarek and Bryan Cranston.

*M*A*S*H*, 1972–1983. Created by Larry Gelbart for CBS. Starring Alan Alda and Wayne Rogers.

Modern Family, 2009–2020. Created by Christopher Lloyd and Steven Levitan for ABC. Starring Ed O'Neill and Sofia Vergara.

The Office U.S., 2005–2013. Created by Greg Daniels for NBC. Starring Steve Carell and Rainn Wilson.

Parks and Recreation, 2009–2015. Created by Greg Daniels and Michael Schur for NBC. Starring Amy Poehler and Rashida Jones.

Scrubs, 2001–2010. Created by Bill Lawrence for ABC and NBC. Starring Zach Braff and Sarah Chalke.

Seinfeld, 1989–1998. Created by Larry David for NBC. Starring Jerry Seinfield and Julia Louis-Dreyfus.

Sex and the City, 1998–2004. Created by Darren Star for HBO. Starring Sarah Jessica Parker and Kim Cattrall.

Will and Grace, 1998–2006, 2017–2020. Created by David Kohan and Max Mutchinick for NBC. Starring Eric McCormack and Debra Messing.

EXAMPLE LIST: AFFIRMATIVE ADJECTIVES

Accomplished	Active	Adaptable	Affectionate	Beautiful
Brave	Bright	Calm	Caring	Charming
Classy	Considerate	Daring	Decisive	Delightful
Dependable	Dynamic	Enchanting	Encouraging	Enthusiastic
Faithful	Fearless	Feisty	Friendly	Generous
Gentle	Glamorous	Goofy	Gracious	Handsome
Humble	Imaginative	Inclusive	Inquisitive	Joyful
Just	Keen	Kind	Kissable	Lighthearted
Lively	Loveable	Loyal	Lucky	Magical
Mature	Mellow	Mysterious	Neat	Nice
Observant	Optimistic	Outgoing	Passionate	Polite
Popular	Powerful	Protective	Quirky	Radiant
Realistic	Receptive	Romantic	Sassy	Sentimental
Shy	Smooth	Spirited	Talented	Talkative
Tender	Thoughtful	Trustworthy	Unbiased	Unique
Upbeat	Vibrant	Vivacious	Warmhearted	Whimsical
Wise	Young	Youthful	Zany	Zappy

BIBLIOGRAPHY

Abello, C. (2021, August 7). *14 Benefits of Being in a Relationship.* Inspiring Tips. https://inspiringtips.com/asia/benefits-of-being-in-a-relationship/

Abgarian, A. (2018, January 29). *10 first-date success stories that will restore your faith in love.* Metro UK. https://metro.co.uk/2018/01/29/10-first-date-success-stories-that-will-restore-your-faith-in-love-7253952/

Ahead of Thyme Incorporated. (2021). *Easy Chicken Parmesan (Parmigiana).* Ahead of Thyme. https://www.aheadofthyme.com/easy-chicken-parmesan-parmigiana/

Butler, C. (2020, November 1). *10 Ways Your Romantic Partner Helps You Reach Your Goals.* Power of Positivity. https://www.powerofpositivity.com/10-ways-your-romantic-partner-helps-you-reach-your-goals/

byjus.com. (2022). *Happy Hormones - Explore the Happy Hormones of the Body.* Byju's. https://byjus.com/biology/happy-hormones/

The Chef & The Dish Inc. (2016, April 25). *The Benefits of Cooking Together.* The Chef & The Dish. https://www.thechefandthedish.com/post/2016/05/18/the-benefits-of-cooking-together

Condé Nast. (2013, July 25). *Why Being in Love Makes You Gorgeous (and Healthy, Too).* Self.com. https://www.self.com/story/sexlove-love-good-for-health-beauty

Connors, C. D. (2019, November 20). *A Little Story on the Remarkable Healing Power of Love.* PS I Love You. https://psiloveyou.xyz/a-little-story-on-the-remarkable-healing-power-of-love-8aad699ef93e

Counselling Directory. (2009, December 14). *Can a relationship survive without intimacy?* Counselling Directory. https://www.counselling-directory.org.uk/memberarticles/can-a-relationship-survive-without-intimacy

Evans, B. (2019, June 28). *25 People Tell Us About The Most Romantic Dates They've Ever Been On*. StyleCaster. https://stylecaster.com/romantic-date-ideas/#slide-6

Fearless Soul. (2020, April 30). *25 Amazing Psychological Facts on Love That Are Backed By Science*. Fearless Soul. https://iamfearlesssoul.com/psychological-facts-on-love/

Finn, C., Mitte, K., & Neyer, F. J. (2015). Recent Decreases in Specific Interpretation Biases Predict Decreases in Neuroticism: Evidence From a Longitudinal Study With Young Adult Couples. *Journal of Personality*, *83*(3), 274-286. Wiley Online Library. 10.1111/jopy.12102

Fisher, H. (2010, February 10). *Why love can make you more creative*. CNN. http://edition.cnn.com/2010/LIVING/personal/02/10/o.love.makes.you.creative/index.html

Förster, J., Epstude, K., & Ozelsel, A. (2018, August 18). Why love has wings and sex has not: how reminders of love and sex influence creative and analytic thinking. *Personality & Social Psychology Bulletin*, *35*(11), 1479-1491. 10.1177/0146167209342755

Gibson, D. (2022). *Why "Date Nights" Matter*. For Your Marriage. https://www.foryourmarriage.org/blogs/why-date-nights-matter/

Goldman, L. (2009, March 9). *The Secret Language of Great Couples*. Women's Health. https://www.womenshealthmag.com/fitness/a19907538/relationship-advice-bond-with-your-guy/

Hughes, S. (2015, October 28). *6 weird facts about sex and love*. Fox News. https://www.foxnews.com/health/6-weird-facts-about-sex-and-love

Issa, C. (2021, February 25). *The Importance of Date Night - OurRelationship*. Our Relationship®. https://www.ourrelationship.com/the-importance-of-date-night/

Jeric, N. (2021, January 22). *21 Love Statistics & Facts to Make Your Heart Skip a Beat*. 2Date4Love. https://2date4love.com/love-statistics/

Kabić, J. (2022, January 17). *30 Amazing Facts And Statistics About Love for 2021*. Review42. https://review42.com/uk/resources/facts-about-love/

Lee, S. (2019, January 10). *3 Easy Couple Dance Steps | Free Dance Tutorial — Online Wedding First Dance Lessons by Duet Dance Studio*. Wedding First Dance Lessons. https://www.weddingfirstdancelessons.com/wedding-dance-blog/easy-couple-dance-steps-dance-tutorial

Legg, T. J. (2020, June 26). *Inner Child: 6 Ways to Find Yours*. Healthline. https://www.healthline.com/health/inner-child#look-to-children

Martell, A. (2014, October 29). *Cooking With Your Spouse Can Strengthen Relationships*. Foodal. https://foodal.com/knowledge/how-to/cooking-spouse-stengthens-relationships/

Moms Who Think. (2022). *Adjectives That Start With A to Z List*. MomsWhoThink.com. https://www.momswhothink.com/adjectives-that-start-with-a-to-z-list/

Moody Publishers. (2022). *The Love Language™ Quiz*. Love Languages. https://5lovelanguages.com/quizzes/love-language

Naik, A. (2011, April 14). *Why marriage is good for your health*. NetDoctor. https://www.netdoctor.co.uk/healthy-living/a10529/why-marriage-is-good-for-your-health/

Nix, T. (2020, September 2). *17 Interesting Facts About Love, which most peoples don't know*. Medium. https://medium.com/illumination/17-interesting-facts-about-love-which-most-peoples-dont-know-3a9eb08d00f1

Northern Homestead. (2022). *7 Proven Steps to Feed a Family on a Tight Budget*. Northern Homestead -. https://northernhomestead.com/feed-a-family-on-a-budget/

Ochs, M. (2022, February 7). *The 100 Best TV Sitcoms of All Time*. Paste Magazine. https://www.pastemagazine.com/tv/the-100-best-tv-sitcoms-of-all-time/

Orr, G. (2017, April 16). *We're Under the Same Roof, But Feel so Distant. Where's Our Intimacy Gone?* Happiful Magazine. https://happiful.com/were-under-the-same-roof-but-feel-so-distant-wheres-our-intimacy-gone/

Our Kind of Crazy. (2022). *12 Ways To Have A Romantic Spa Date Night At Home*. Our Kind of Crazy. https://ourkindofcrazy.com/blog/spa-date-night-at-home/

Pugachevsky, J., & Andrews, T. (2020, April 29). *Personality Quizzes to Take With Your Partner - Couple Compatibility Tests to Try.* Cosmopolitan. https://www.cosmopolitan.com/sex-love/a26750731/relationship-dating-compatibility-personality-tests/

RelRules.com. (2018, December 22). *If You've Found This Person, Then Consider Yourself Lucky.* RelRules. https://www.relrules.com/if-youve-found-this-person-then-consider-yourself-lucky/

Shah, N. (2016, January 28). *What's the link between stress and poor health?* The Stress Management Society. https://www.stress.org.uk/whats-the-link-between-stress-and-poor-health/

Tanzi, A. (2019, October 9). *Marriage Leads to a Longer Life, at Least Until Your Spouse Dies.* Bloomberg.com. https://www.bloomberg.com/news/articles/2019-10-10/marriage-leads-to-a-longer-life-at-least-until-your-spouse-dies

Television Food Network. (2017). *Steakhouse Sheet Pan Dinner for Two Recipe | Food Network Kitchen.* Food Network. https://www.foodnetwork.com/recipes/food-network-kitchen/steakhouse-sheet-pan-dinner-for-two-4481581

Television Food Network. (2021). *Risotto with Lemon and Shrimp for Two Recipe.* Food Network. https://www.foodnetwork.com/recipes/risotto-with-lemon-and-shrimp-for-two-3416117

Thomas, Y., Wertheim, G., & Adkins, Z. (2022, April 10). *4 Ways to Learn to Dance at Home.* wikiHow. https://www.wikihow.com/Learn-to-Dance-at-Home

University of Utah Health - Office of Public Affairs. (2017, February 14). *Seven Reasons Why Loving Relationships Are Good For You.* University of Utah Health. https://healthcare.utah.edu/healthfeed/postings/2017/02/relationships.php

Upreti, G. (n.d.). *Adventurous Couple Travel Story, Meaning of True Love.* Tripoto. Retrieved 2022, from https://www.tripoto.com/new-york/trips/this-adventurous-couple-traveled-the-world-and-finally-found-the-meaning-of-true-love-408269

BIBLIOGRAPHY | 197

Velez, A. (2018, February 14). *17 First Date Stories That Are So Pure And Wonderful, You Might Not Recover.* BuzzFeed. https://www.buzzfeed.com/alivelez/17-first-date-stories-that-will-remind-you-romance-is-alive

Villalon, C. (2021, March 28). *14 Characteristics of a Healthy Relationship.* Inspiring Tips. https://inspiringtips.com/characteristics-of-a-healthy-relationship/

Wellness Living Systems Inc. (2020, January 9). *2020 Dance Trends You Need to Know.* WellnessLiving. https://www.wellnessliving.com/blog/2020-dance-trends-dance-management-software/

White, T. (2010, October 13). *Love takes up where pain leaves off, brain study shows.* Stanford Medicine. https://med.stanford.edu/news/all-news/2010/10/love-takes-up-where-pain-leaves-off-brain-study-shows.html

wikiHow. (2022, May 30). *4 Ways to Make Your Own Secret Language.* wikiHow. https://www.wikihow.com/Make-Your-Own-Secret-Language

Wilbert, C., & Chang, L. (2009, November 20). *Photo of a Loved One Reduces Pain.* WebMD. https://www.webmd.com/pain-management/news/20091120/photo-of-a-loved-one-reduces-pain

Worldometers.info. (2022). *United States Population (2022).* Worldometer. https://www.worldometers.info/world-population/us-population/

Worldometers.info. (2022). *World Population by Year.* Worldometer. https://www.worldometers.info/world-population/world-population-by-year/

Made in United States
Troutdale, OR
03/21/2025